MAKE-U & JEWELLERY

GW00858987

PART ONE   MAKE-UP

Felicity Everett

Illustrated by Conny Jude

Consultant: Saskia Sarginson

Designed by Camilla Luff

Edited by Angela Wilkes

CONTENTS

About make-up

Make-up is exciting and colourful. You can wear as much, or as little, as you like. The important thing is to wear make-up which suits you and is right for the occasion.

This book shows you how to choose and put on make-up. It also gives you lots of ideas for ways to vary the basic looks in the book and invent some of your own.

Your make-up kit

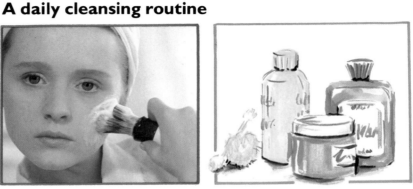

Before you begin to experiment with make-up, you need to collect your make-up kit.

A few simple items go a long way. You can find out which basic things you need on pages 8-9.

Skincare

You can find out what kind of skin you have, and how to look after it on pages 4-5.

A daily cleansing routine

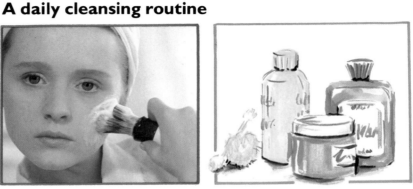

A really effective cleansing routine is important if you wear make-up. On pages 6-7, there is a

daily cleansing routine you can follow, and a table telling you which products suit your skin.

Choosing colours

Turn to page 10 for some hints on which make-up shades might flatter your colouring.

Shaping and shading with colours

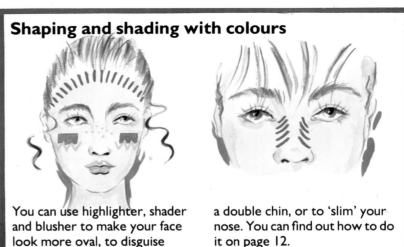

You can use highlighter, shader and blusher to make your face look more oval, to disguise

a double chin, or to 'slim' your nose. You can find out how to do it on page 12.

A perfect make-up

The make-up techniques in part one are illustrated step-by-step so you know exactly what to do.

Handy hints

Pictures in boxes this shape and size give tips on how to apply your make-up better.

The natural look

On page 18, you can find out how to do a natural-looking make-up, with the minimum of fuss.

Top-to-toe beauty treatment

The beauty routine on pages 20-23 includes conditioning treatments for your hair.

There are also recipes for home-made face masks using natural ingredients.

You can see how to give your hands a manicure and there are lots more ideas too.

Bright ideas for party make-up

From page 24 onwards, you will find some colourful and original ideas for party make-up.

The step-by-step instructions are as detailed as before, but the results are more dramatic.

Nostalgic looks

On pages 30-31, you can find out how to re-create nostalgic make-up looks from the past.

Looking after your skin

It is important to look after your skin properly, especially if you wear make-up.

To keep it healthy, you should cleanse and moisturise it each day. You will need:

Cleanser is cream or lotion which you use to clean your skin and take off your make-up. You can see how to do it on pages 6-7.

Moisturiser is cream or lotion which protects and softens your skin and stops it from becoming too dry. You can see how to put it on over the page.

Toner is liquid which closes up the pores after you have cleansed your skin and freshens it.

You can use a **cleansing bar** instead of cleanser, if your skin is oily. This looks like ordinary soap, but will not dry your skin.

Eye make-up remover can be liquid, or ready-to-use pads. It removes eye make-up gently.

Cotton buds are good for touching your face without making it greasy.

Cotton wool and tissues are useful for taking off your make-up and for putting on creams and lotions.

Diet

For clear healthy skin, eat plenty of fresh fruit and vegetables and drink lots of water. Don't eat sweets.

What skin type are you?

Look for skin care products which are recommended for your type of skin. If you don't know what type yours is, the simple test below will tell you whether your skin is dry, oily or normal. All you need is a roll of sticky tape.

Press a piece of sticky tape lightly over the bridge of your nose and on to your cheeks, avoiding the area round your eyes. Pull it off and look at it.

white flakes = dry skin
drops of moisture = oily skin
both = normal skin

Problem skin

If you often get rashes, look for hypo-allergenic products. They are made from pure ingredients which should not irritate your skin.

If you get lots of spots, use medicated skin products. *Never* squeeze spots. If you have a bad one, dab it gently with a cotton bud soaked in lemon juice.

KEY

DRY SKIN

OILY SKIN

Dry skin

Usually affects cheeks most – causes flaky patches, makes skin feel 'tight', after washing.

Oily skin

Often looks slightly shiny – usually affects nose, chin and forehead, sometimes tends to be spotty.

Normal skin

Dry in parts and oily in others – also called combination skin.

Cleansing

Follow this simple cleansing routine every morning* and evening.

1   Removing eye make-up

Apply make-up remover with cotton wool. Gently stroke it downwards and inwards towards the corner of each eye, making sure you do not pull the skin around your eyes.

2   Cleansing

If you use a cleansing bar, lather your face with a shaving brush, then rinse it off. Or you can smooth cream cleanser over your face and neck, then wipe it off gently with a tissue.

Finding the right products for your skin

This chart shows you which creams and lotions suit different types of skin.

To find out what type of skin you have, do the simple test on page 5.

Skin type	Cleanser	Toner	Moisturiser
Dry skin	Cream or thick liquid cleanser.	Mild toner: camomile, rose water, or still mineral water.	cream moisturiser.
Oily skin	Lotion or cleansing milk.	Natural astringent, such as witch hazel or cucumber.	Light, non-greasy liquid moisturiser.
Combination skin	Creamy liquid or cream cleanser.	Mild toner: camomile, rosewater or still mineral water.	Thin cream or thick lotion.

3 Toning

Soak a cotton wool pad in toner and gently wipe it over your face. Or you can put the toner into an atomiser (an old, clean perfume spray would do) and spray it over your face.

4 Moisturising

Put little dots of moisturiser over your face and neck and gently rub it into your skin with your fingertips. You can put more on areas which are especially dry, such as your cheeks.

Deep cleansing

Deep cleansing about once a fortnight helps to keep your skin soft and really clean.

Any of the methods shown below work well. Used together, they make an excellent facial.

Facial sauna

Fill a big bowl with boiling water. Hold your face about 20cm from the water and drape a towel over your head to stop steam from escaping. Wait for five minutes.

Facial scrubs

Facial scrubs (or exfoliating creams) contain tiny granules which rub off the top layer of skin. Read the instructions on the packet for what to do.

Face masks*

You can buy gels, creams, or mud-based masks. Choose one which is recommended for your type of skin. Read the instructions on the packet for what to do.

* You will find some recipes for home-made face masks on page 21.

Your make-up kit

Here are the things you need to do a complete make-up, like the one on pages 14-17.

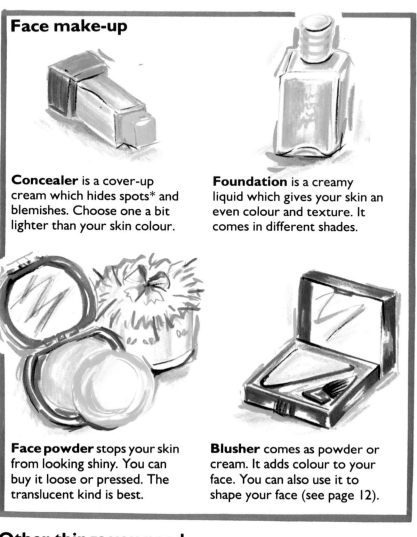

Face make-up

Concealer is a cover-up cream which hides spots* and blemishes. Choose one a bit lighter than your skin colour.

Foundation is a creamy liquid which gives your skin an even colour and texture. It comes in different shades.

Face powder stops your skin from looking shiny. You can buy it loose or pressed. The translucent kind is best.

Blusher comes as powder or cream. It adds colour to your face. You can also use it to shape your face (see page 12).

Lips

Lipstick adds colour and moisture to your lips. To put it on properly you need a lip pencil and a lip brush.

Lip gloss can be worn over lipstick, or on its own. It makes your lips look shiny and stops them from chapping.

Other things you need

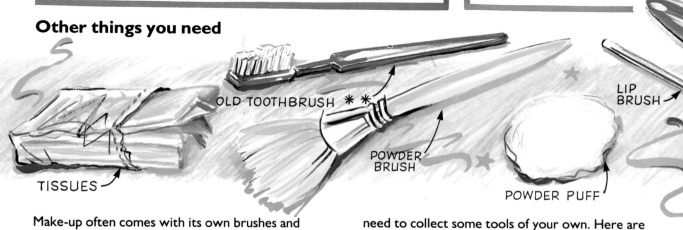

OLD TOOTHBRUSH **

LIP BRUSH →

POWDER BRUSH

TISSUES

POWDER PUFF

Make-up often comes with its own brushes and applicators, but for a really professional look, you will need to collect some tools of your own. Here are some useful ones to start off with.

8   * You can buy medicated concealer especially for spots.   ** For combing your eyebrows.

Eye make-up

Eye-shadows come in different forms. To start with, choose two matching pressed powder eye-shadows.

You can also buy eye-shadow in pots (of powder or cream), in tubes (of cream), or in pencils (of powder or cream).

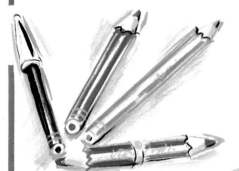

Eye pencil is for outlining your eyes, close to your eyelashes. Choose one a shade darker than your eye-shadow.

Mascara is thick liquid for darkening your eyelashes, you put it on with a brush. Use black or brown for everyday.

Professional make-up tips

Do not lend your make-up to anyone, even your best friend. You can pass on eye infections and cold sores.

To check that your foundation is the right colour for you, test it on your face (without any make-up on).

Keep your pencils sharp. You can sharpen them better if you put them in the fridge for an hour before you need them.

Keep your make-up in a clean, dry place. A box with compartments, such as a plastic tool box is ideal.

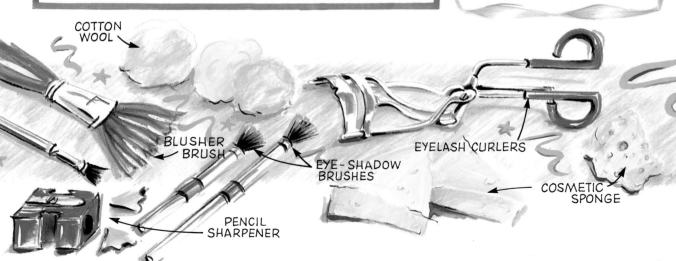

COTTON WOOL

BLUSHER BRUSH

EYE-SHADOW BRUSHES

EYELASH CURLERS

COSMETIC SPONGE

PENCIL SHARPENER

Choosing colours

It is fun trying out make-up colours, but mistakes can be expensive. It is best to choose shades which go with your colouring.

Here are six typical hair and skin colours. Below each picture, you can see the make-up colours which flatter that type.

Fair skin/brown hair

Brunettes often have fair skin and rosy cheeks. If your skin looks blotchy, even it out with a creamy-beige foundation.

Fair skin/blonde hair

Blondes have fair, rather dry skin which needs careful skin care. Use a pinkish foundation to give colour to your skin.

Freckled skin/red hair

Redheads tend to have fair, sensitive, freckled skin. Choose a light foundation which lets your freckles show through.

Blusher

TAWNY PINK

GOLDEN PEACH

Eyes

GRASS GREEN
SAND BROWN
APRICOT
GOLD
BLUE

Lips

PALE PINK   CORAL   RICH RED

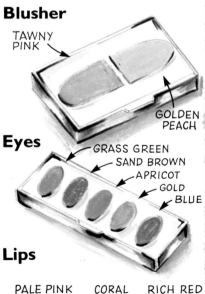

Blusher

BEIGE PINK

PEACH

Eyes

CORNFLOWER BLUE
PINKY MAUVE
SOFT BROWN
VIOLET
GREY

Lips

SUGAR PINK   PEACH BROWN   WARM PINK

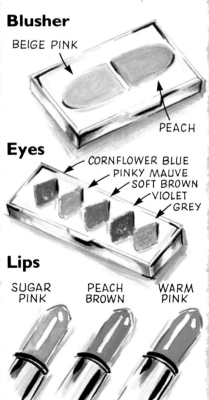

Blusher

AMBER

DUSKY PINK

Eyes

GOLDEN BROWN
SAGE GREEN
TAWNY PINK
PLUM
RUST

Lips

PALE PEACH   BURGUNDY   RASPBERRY

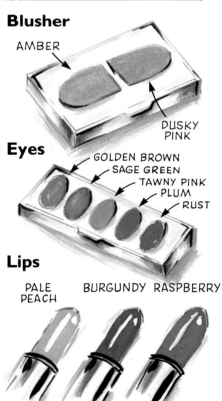

10

Several companies make foundations and concealers especially for dark skin. You can mix two colours together if you cannot find the right shade.

Do not wear powder. It will just make your skin look dull. Let it's natural sheen show through a light coating of foundation.

Black skin/dark hair

Black skin can be oily and sometimes the colour is a little uneven. Even it out with a light, non-greasy foundation.

Brown skin/dark hair

Brown skin can be slightly blotchy. Mix foundation and concealer and then use the mixture to even out your colouring.

Olive skin/dark hair

Olive skin can look sallow and may be oily, but a non-greasy, dark beige foundation can make it look healthy and golden.

Blusher

BRICK RED

BURGUNDY

Eyes

GOLDEN BROWN
BUTTERCUP
NAVY BLUE
ORANGE
ROSE

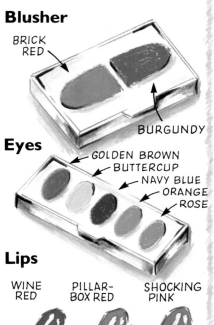

Lips

WINE RED

PILLAR-BOX RED

SHOCKING PINK

Blusher

GOLDEN BROWN

MAUVE

Eyes

TAWNY GOLD
YELLOW
MAUVE
BLUE
PLUM

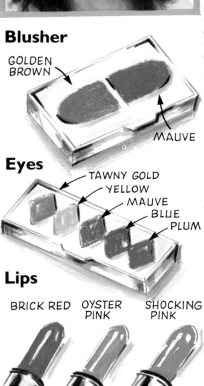

Lips

BRICK RED

OYSTER PINK

SHOCKING PINK

Blusher

COPPER

BURGUNDY

Eyes

PINKY BEIGE
MOSS GREEN
FRENCH NAVY
GOLD
PLUM

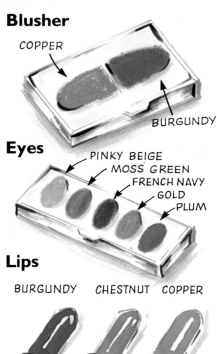

Lips

BURGUNDY

CHESTNUT

COPPER

Shaping and shading

Here you can find out how to use shader, highlighter and blusher to make your face look more oval, and show off your best features.

It is best to wear shader and highlighter in the evenings. They can look too obvious during the day.

The key below shows you exactly where to put your highlighter, shader and blusher. Blend them in well, so no hard edges show.

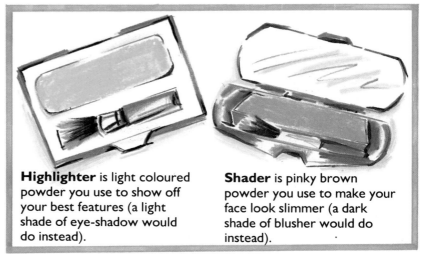

Highlighter is light coloured powder you use to show off your best features (a light shade of eye-shadow would do instead).

Shader is pinky brown powder you use to make your face look slimmer (a dark shade of blusher would do instead).

What shape is your face?

LONG FACE

ROUND FACE

HEART-SHAPED FACE

SQUARE FACE

KEY
SHADER   /////
HIGHLIGHTER VVV
BLUSHER   ▬

Pull your hair back from your face and look at it in the mirror. Compare your face shape with the four basic shapes shown here. Then look at the key to find out where to put your highlighter, shader and blusher.

Shader

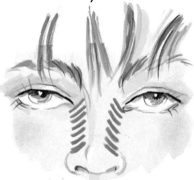

To make your cheekbones look higher, suck in your cheeks and dot shader in the hollows below them. Blend it in from your cheeks towards your hairline.

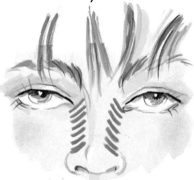

To make your nose look slimmer, dot a little shader down each side of it, or wherever your nose is uneven. Blend it in evenly with the tip of your finger.

To disguise a double chin, dab a little shader just beneath your chin and blend it in well around your jawline. Make sure it does not look like a dirty tide mark.

Highlighter

To highlight high cheekbones, dot a little highlighter just above your cheekbones and blend it in evenly, so it slants upwards towards your hairline.

If you have attractive eyes, dab a little highlighter on to each browbone (the area just beneath your eyebrows). Blend it in so that it barely shows.

If your mouth is your best feature, use a lip brush to stroke a little highlighter into the dimple above your top lip. Blend it in evenly so it barely shows.

Blusher

You can use blusher to give your face a better shape, as well as to give it colour. Blend it in to your highlighter and shader so that no hard lines show.

To give a hint of colour to your whole face, dot a little blusher on to each earlobe, as shown. Then blend it in well with your brush, so it barely shows.

If you are looking pale, dab a little blusher around your hairline, as shown. Then blend it in thoroughly so there is just a hint of colour showing.

Step-by-step to a perfect make-up

Getting ready

Put your make-up on in a room with a good-sized mirror and lots of light. You can find out what make-up you need on pages 8-9.

Tie your hair out of the way, or put on a headband. Wash your face and put on moisturiser. Now you are ready to begin.

Concealer

Dot a little concealer over any spots, blemishes or dark shadows and blend it in well with the tip of your finger.

Foundation

Dot a little foundation over your face. Put it over your lips too, but not your eyelids, as it will make them oily.

Wet your cosmetic sponge in warm water, then squeeze most of the water out and blot it on a piece of tissue.

Use the sponge to spread the foundation evenly over your face. Make sure you smooth it in well under your chin.

Powder

Dip a ball of cotton wool into your tub of loose powder, then pat it firmly, but gently all over your face until it is evenly covered.

Use a large, soft powder brush to flick off the spare powder. Brush it downwards to make the tiny hairs on your face lie flat.

If a stubborn spot still shows through foundation and powder, dab a clean brush on your concealer and paint it out.

14

Blusher

Stroke your blusher brush across your palette of powder blusher until it is lightly, but evenly, coated with powder.

Brush the blusher on to your cheekbones (this is the area just above your cheeks), and right up to your hairline.

Keep adding more until the colour is strong enough. If it starts to look too obvious, you can tone it down with powder.

Professional make-up tips

To find out what colour blusher you need, lightly pinch the skin on your cheeks. The colour which appears is the shade of blusher you need.

Do not put your make-up on straight after a bath or shower as your skin is more flushed than usual. Wait until it cools down and returns to normal.

You can re-cycle old lipstick ends by heating them in a bowl over a pan of boiling water. Put the mixture in a pot to go solid. Put it on with a brush.

To make your eyelashes look extra thick, dust them with face powder then brush away the excess, before you put on your mascara.

Check your finished face make-up to make sure there are no hard lines of colour anywhere.

If you can see any, blend them in with a brush. Now you are ready to make up your eyes and lips.

15

Eyes

Eye-shadow

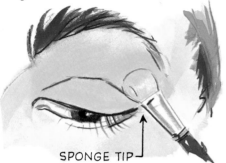

SPONGE TIP

Start by stroking the lighter shade of eye-shadow over your eyelids, as shown. Blend it in with an eye-shadow brush.

Stroke the darker shade of eye-shadow on to the outer half of your eyelids, as shown. Blend in the edges with another brush.

Brushing eyebrows

Brush your eyebrows upwards with an old toothbrush. Then smooth them in the direction they grow, with your fingertip.

Eye pencil

Draw a fine pencil line along your eyelids, next to your lashes, as shown. Smudge the line slightly with a damp cotton bud.

Draw another line underneath your eyes, close to your lower lashes, as shown, and smudge it gently, as before.

If you want to put pencil on the inner rim of your eye, use one which is not too sharp and draw it on carefully.

Curling eyelashes

Clamp the eyelash curlers round your top lashes very carefully. Hold them shut for a minute, then open them again.

Mascara

Look into a hand mirror, held at chin level. Brush mascara on to your top lashes. Let it dry, then put on a second coat.

Look straight ahead into your make-up mirror to put mascara on your bottom lashes. You only need to put on one coat.

16

Lips

Outlining your lips

Draw an outline around the edge of your mouth with a lip pencil, resting your little finger on your chin to steady your hand.

You can use a fine lip brush to outline your mouth, if you want. Dab it on your lipstick, then paint in the outline.

Putting on lipstick

Coat your lip brush with colour from your lipstick. Carefully paint the colour on to your lips, keeping within the outline.

Blotting your lipstick

Blot your lipstick on a tissue (taking care not to smudge it). Then put on a second coat and blot your lips again.

Lip gloss

To give your lips some shine, dot lip gloss in the centre of your lips and carefully brush it outwards towards the edges.

This make-up is good for evenings, when you want to make a special effort to look good.

Allow plenty of time to do it. You can see how to do a quick, simple make-up over the page.

The natural look

All you need for a simple, natural looking make-up* are the things shown here.

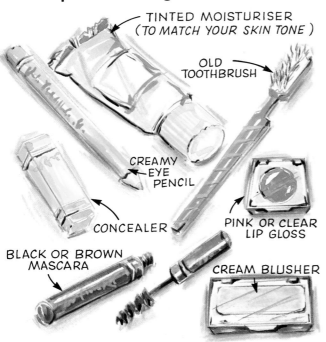

TINTED MOISTURISER
(TO MATCH YOUR SKIN TONE)

OLD
TOOTHBRUSH

CREAMY
EYE
PENCIL

CONCEALER

PINK OR CLEAR
LIP GLOSS

BLACK OR BROWN
MASCARA

CREAM BLUSHER

1 Concealer and tinted moisturiser

Tie your hair back. Wash your face and pat it dry. Cover any blemishes with concealer (see page 14). Dot moisturiser on with your finger and smooth it in.

2 Blusher

Use your fingertips to dot blusher on to your cheeks, then carefully smooth the blusher outwards and upwards towards your hairline.

3 Eye pencil

Carefully draw a pencil line across your eyelid, next to your eyelashes. Then smooth the colour over your eyelid, using a damp cotton bud, or your fingertip.

*This make-up goes well with the natural jewellery on pages 42-45 and the pretty jewellery on pages 46-51.

4 Mascara

Brush mascara on to your upper lashes, as on page 16, let it dry and then apply a second coat. Brush one coat of mascara on to your lower lashes.

5 Brushing your eyebrows

Use an old toothbrush to brush your eyebrows upwards. Then wet your finger and smooth it over each eyebrow in the direction it grows.

6 Lip gloss

Using a lip brush, paint lip gloss carefully on to your lips. Do not brush it right to the edge of your mouth, as it can 'run' and look rather messy.

7 The finished look

This is what the finished make-up should look like. With a bit of practise, you will be able to do it in a matter of minutes.

Top-to-toe beauty routine

If you are planning a special night out and want to look and feel your best, give yourself an all-over beauty treatment, following this step-by-step plan.

Set aside a few hours (you will need at least two) so that you can relax and really enjoy yourself. If you are going out with a friend, you could ask her over so you can have fun getting ready together.

Having a bath

Run a warm bath, adding some moisturising bath oil or bubble bath. Do not spend longer than twenty minutes soaking, or your skin will start to wrinkle.

While you are in the bath, take a handful of coarse sea salt and rub it over your bottom and thighs to stimulate your circulation and make you tingle.

Then massage your skin all over with a textured bath mitt. Its rough surface will rub off any dead skin and leave your body feeling soft and smooth.

Get out of the bath and pat yourself dry with a soft towel. Dust some talc over your feet and under your arms (use deodorant under your arms, if you prefer).

Massage a moisturising body lotion all over your body (if your skin is dry, use body oil). Pay special attention to dry skin on your heels and elbows.

Conditioning your hair

Warm two tablespoons of olive oil or almond oil in a saucepan (do not let it get too hot, or it will scald you). Massage it into your hair until it is all absorbed.

Wrap a piece of clingfilm around your hair, overlapping it at the front. Scrunch it up to seal the ends together. Make sure you do not drip oil on your clothes.

Then wrap a warm towel round your head in a turban. Leave it on for thirty minutes. You can see how to wash out the oil on the next page.

Putting on a face mask

While your hair conditioner is working, put on a face mask (see below for recipes). You can find out how to do this on page 7.

You can put thin slices of cucumber or potato on your eyes if you like. This soothes them.

Put on some soothing music, lie back and relax for ten minutes. Then rinse off the face mask with warm water and pat your face dry with a soft towel.

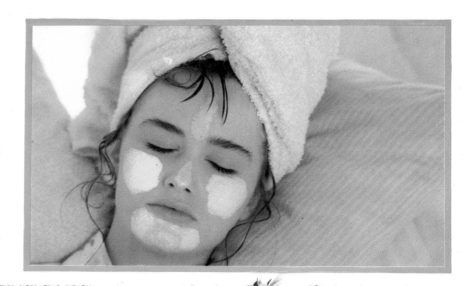

Home-made face masks

For dry skin: mix together a tablespoon of plain yogurt, a teaspoon of runny honey and a mashed, ripe avocado. Spread the mixture on your face and leave it on for ten to fifteen minutes.

For oily skin: mix together a tablespoon of plain yogurt, a teaspoon of honey, a teaspoon of oatmeal and a mashed peach. Spread it on your face and leave for ten minutes.

For normal skin: crush a few thick slices of cucumber to a pulp and mix them with a teaspoon of plain yogurt and a few drops of rose water. Spread the mixture on your face and leave it on for fifteen minutes.

Removing unwanted hair

Everyone has hair on their legs, but there is no need to remove it unless you really want to.

Depilatory cream is the gentlest and easiest method of removing hair. It is safer than shaving and less painful than waxing your legs.

If you decide to remove the hair on your legs, it is best to remove it regularly. The hairs that grow back look thicker, because they are short and stubbly.

Read the instructions on the packet before you start. Squeeze some cream into the palm of your hand, then spread it thickly over your legs with your fingers.

Leave it on for as long as the packet tells you to. Then wipe it off gently with a wet cloth. Rinse your legs and then pat them dry with a towel.

Washing your hair

When your conditioning hair oil has been on for half an hour, wash it off. Shampoo your hair twice and rinse it thoroughly to remove every trace of the oil.

Comb your hair very gently to remove any tangles. Start at the ends of your hair and work back towards your head. Do not tug the comb through clumps of your hair.

If you are blow drying your hair, do it in sections. Hold the hair dryer at least ten cm from your hair and keep it moving, as you dry, to avoid damaging your hair.

Styling your hair

You can buy soft, fabric hair curlers like the ones in the photograph which will curl your hair without damaging it. You can make corkscrew curls or soft waves.

Put them in your hair and leave them for 45 minutes. Meanwhile you can give yourself a manicure and pedicure (see below and opposite).

When you take the curlers out, gently brush your hair, or just run your fingers through it, to separate the curls.

Your hands

Treat your hands to a manicure before you go out. First, file your nails with an emery board. It is best to file from the edges to the centre of your nails.

Then soak your fingertips in warm, soapy water for a few minutes. If your nails are dirty, scrub them with a nailbrush. Dry your hands. Then rub on some hand cream.

Rub some cuticle cream into the hard pads of skin at the base of your nails to soften them. Then gently push back the cuticle with a cotton bud.

Carefully paint on a thin coat of nail varnish. There are some ideas for party nails on page 25. When the varnish is dry, carefully put on another coat.

Your feet

Now you can give yourself a pedicure. Trim your toenails straight across with nail clippers. Then file them from the edges inwards.

Soften your cuticles with cream and push them back. Then separate your toes with cotton wool* and put on two coats of varnish.

Plucking your eyebrows

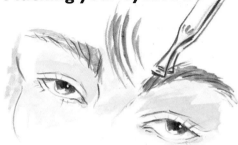

Before you put your make-up on, tidy your eyebrows by plucking any straggly hairs that grow beneath them. Pluck them in the direction they grow.

Make-up

Now you can put on your make-up. First, tie your hair back and put some moisturiser on your face. Then, turn to pages 24 to 31 for some ideas on party make-up.

Scent

If you wear scent, such as toilet water or perfume, dab a little on your pulse points (behind your ears and knees and on the inside of your wrists and elbows).

Ready to go

Now you can get dressed. Make sure you don't spoil your hair or smudge your make-up. Check your appearance in a full length mirror before you go out.

* You can buy foam toe pads from the chemists, which do the same thing.

Party make-up

Party make-up can be anything from bold eyeshadow and bright lipstick, to false eyelashes, sequins and turquoise mascara. Here are some things to collect.

CHILDREN'S FACE PAINTS

STAGE MAKE - UP *

NAIL VARNISH IN UNUSUAL COLOURS

FALSE EYELASHES

SEQUINS AND STARS

Eye-shadows

You can buy little pots of loose, sparkly powder eye-shadow in lots of colours. To stop it from spilling on to your cheeks, put it on with a damp brush.

Mascara

You can buy mascara in lots of bright colours, such as violet and green. If you want a hint of colour, brush it on to the tips of your lashes only.

Eyebrows

You can colour your eyebrows to match your mascara. Dab a little mascara on your eyebrow brush. Blot the brush on a tissue, then brush your eyebrows with it.

False eye-lashes

Put these on before your eye-shadow. Apply a coat of mascara, then dot eyelash glue along the lash band with a pin. Make sure you glue each end.

Let the glue dry for a second. Then pick up the lashes with a pair of tweezers and position them on your closed eyelid, on top of your real lashes.

Gently press the lash band down on to your eyelid with your finger. Wait for the glue to dry, then brush the eyelashes upwards with an old toothbrush.

* If you have difficulty finding stage make-up, you can write to Charles Fox Ltd, theatre make-up suppliers, 22 Tavistock St, London WC2.

FROSTED BLUSHER

SHIMMERY POWDER EYE-SHADOW

COLOURED MASCARA

GLITTER DUST

TEMPORARY HAIR COLOUR

Designer finger nails

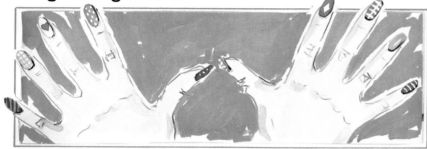

Manicure your nails as on page 22. Then put on nail varnish. You can buy it in lots of bright colours. Use two or more colours to paint on spots, stripes, checks or any design you like. If you are using more than one colour, make sure each coat is thoroughly dry before you apply the next, or your nail varnish will smudge.

Glitter dust and sequins

You can make shimmery lip gloss by mixing some glitter dust with your ordinary lip gloss in the palm of your hand. Then brush it on your lips, in the usual way.

Add shine to your make-up by glueing sequins on your face with eyelash glue. Put them at the outer corners of your eyes, or glue one on as a beauty spot.

Colouring your hair

You can change your hair colour for the evening, using a wash in/wash out hair colour mousse or shampoo, in an unusual colour.

Another way of adding flashes of colour to your hair, is to attach thin swatches of false hair to your own, using slides or ribbons.

25

Polka dot make-up

This party make-up combines the sophistication of black and white with the fun of polka dots for a stunning effect.

You will need

light beige foundation
translucent powder
white and dark grey powder eye-
  shadows
black eye pencil
black mascara
pale pink or white lipstick
matching lip pencil

Foundation

First, smooth foundation all over your face and neck, using a cosmetic sponge. You can check the techniques for applying this make-up, on pages 14-17.

Powder

Then powder your face quite thickly using a cotton wool ball, or a powder puff and gently flick off any spare powder with your powder brush.

Eye-shadow

Brush a thick layer of white eye-shadow over the whole of your eyelid, as shown. You may need two coats to get the heavy, matt effect shown here.

Then brush dark grey eye-shadow along the line of your eye socket as shown, broadening the line towards the outer corner of your eye. Blend it in with a brush.

Eye pencil

Sharpen your eye pencil until you get a really good point. Then, warm the tip of your pencil in the palm of your hand, so it goes on thickly.

Draw pencil dots on your eyelids, as shown. Press firmly but gently with the tip of the pencil, turning it slightly at the same time, so the dots show up well.

Carefully draw a fine black pencil line along your eyelid, close to your upper eyelashes. Then smudge it slightly with a damp cotton bud, or your finger.

Mascara

Curl your eyelashes with eyelash curlers, then brush mascara on to your upper lashes. Let it dry, then put on a second coat. Put one coat on your lower lashes.

Brushing eyebrows

Brush your eyebrows with your eyebrow brush. Then dip the tip of your finger in a little Vaseline and smooth it over your eyebrows to make them shine.

Lipstick

Outline your lips with a fine brush, or a lip pencil which matches your lipstick. Then put on your lipstick. Blot it on a tissue, apply another coat and blot again.

Too pale?

If you think your finished make-up looks too pale, brush on a little pink blusher. Make sure you blend it in well.

Hair

If you have short hair, smooth it back with hair gel. If your hair is long, tie it back, then tie a scarf round your head in a big, floppy bow, as shown.

If you have a fringe, put setting lotion on it, then use curling tongs to make it wavy. Comb it upwards and spray hair spray on it to make it stand up.

This make-up looks especially good worn with black and white clothes and the black and white speckled jewellery on page 55. There is another quite different party make-up on the next page.

27

Razzle dazzle make-up

You are sure to be noticed in this colourful party make-up. You can use different colours from the ones shown here if you like.

You will need

foundation
translucent powder
golden peach blusher
orange, sea green and smoky
  grey eye-shadows
black and emerald green mascara
orange lipstick
matching lip pencil and lip brush
gold lip gloss

Foundation

First, smooth foundation all over your face and neck, using a cosmetic sponge. You can check the techniques for putting on make-up on pages 14-17.

Powder

Then powder your face lightly all over, using a cotton wool ball or a powder puff. Gently flick off any loose powder with your powder brush.

Blusher

Brush blusher on to your cheeks, as shown. You can put on a little more in the evening than you would during the day, but make sure you blend it in well.

Eye-shadow

Brush orange eye-shadow on to the inner half of one eyelid and the outer half of the other eyelid. You can put on quite a lot, as long as you blend it in well.

Brush green eye-shadow on to the other half of each eyelid and blend it in well where it meets the orange eyeshadow, so that the two colours merge.

Dampen a fine tipped brush and use it to stroke grey eye-shadow in a fine line along your upper lash line and at the outer corners of the lower lashes.

Mascara

Brush black mascara on to your upper and lower eye lashes (you can see how on page 16). When it is dry, brush a second coat on your upper lashes.

Brush emerald green mascara carefully on to the tips of your eyelashes. If you want a stronger shade of green, wait for it to dry, then put on a second coat.

Brushing eyebrows

Brush your eyebrows upwards (you can put a little brown eye-shadow on the brush if you want to darken them). Then smooth them with your finger.

Lipstick

Outline your lips with your orange lip pencil (or a lip brush coated with lipstick). Fill in the colour with your orange lipstick and a lip brush keeping within the outline.

Lip gloss

Brush a little gold lip gloss on to the middle of your lower lip to make your lips look fuller. You could use non-toxic gold eye-shadow instead.

Hair

If you have long hair which is not naturally curly, curl it as on page 22. Then tie a brightly coloured scarf round your head in a big, floppy bow.

If you have a fringe, pull a few wispy strands of it down in front of your eyes and then gently finger a little hair gel through it to separate the curls.

This razzle dazzle make-up looks especially good worn with the bright jewellery on pages 36-41 of part two.

You could match your eyeshadow shades with the colours in your jewellery to create a really striking effect.

Four nostalgic looks

Here you can find out how to create some distinctive make-up looks from the twenties, forties, fifties and sixties.

You can dress the part, too, whether it's for a special party with a nostalgic theme, or just for fun.

The 1920s

In the 1920s girls wore bold eye make-up, bright lipstick and sometimes a false beauty spot. They often had their hair bobbed.

You will need: pale foundation, translucent powder, dark eye-shadow, black mascara, dark eyebrow pencil, glossy pink or red lipstick and a matching lip pencil or lip brush.

Face: put on your foundation and powder.

Eyes: brush eye-shadow over your eyelids and browbones. Smudge a little under your lower lashes. Then put on lots of mascara. Pencil in narrow, arched eyebrows.

Lips: were painted in a very distinctive shape in the twenties. Outline them with lip pencil to emphasize your 'Cupid's Bow' (the dimple in your top lip). Then put on your lipstick, being careful to keep within the outline.

Finally, paint or stick on a false beauty spot, as shown.

The 1940s

Make-up was bold and glamorous in the 1940s. Girls painted on dark eyebrows and bright red lips. They often wore their hair elegantly rolled at the front, and left the back loose round their shoulders.

You will need: pale foundation, translucent powder, dark blusher (in brown or plum), grey or brown eye pencil, eyebrow pencil, glossy red lipstick and matching lip pencil, or a lip brush.

Face: put on your foundation and powder. Brush blusher high on your cheekbones.

Eyes: brush eye-shadow on your eyelids, close to your eyelashes. Put mascara on your top lashes only. Thicken and darken your eyebrows with eyebrow pencil.

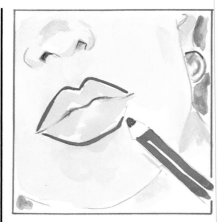

Lips: outline them carefully with your lip pencil, squaring off the bottom lip slightly, as shown. Then paint them with two or three coats of lipstick, keeping within the outline. Blot your lips between each coat, so your lipstick will stay on longer.

The 1950s

Fifties make-up concentrated on the eyes. Black eyeliner swept up at the corners gave eyes a cat-like look. Girls wore their hair in high pony tails, with the front rolled, or worn in a short, neat fringe.

You will need: light beige foundation, slightly lighter powder, pink blusher, light blue or yellow eye-shadow, liquid eyeliner, a few false eyelashes, eyelash glue, mascara, pink lip pencil and pale pink pearly lipstick.

Face: put on your foundation, powder and blusher.

Eyes: brush eye-shadow on to your eyelids. Carefully paint a narrow line of liquid eyeliner close to your top eyelashes, winging it upwards slightly at the outer corners of your eyes.

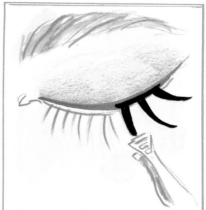

Cut small sections off complete false eyelashes and stick them at the outer corners of your eyes with eyelash glue, as shown. Brush two coats of mascara on to your upper lashes only.

Lips: outline them with lip pencil and fill in with lipstick.

The 1960s

Girls in the 1960s wore a lot of dark eye make-up. Faces and lips were as pale as possible. Girls wore their hair in short, boyish haircuts, or backcombed into a glamorous 'bouffant' style.

You will need: pale foundation and powder, pale matt eye-shadow (pink or white), grey eye pencil, black liquid eyeliner, false eyelashes, eyelash glue, black eye pencil, black mascara, pale matt lipstick.

Face: put on your foundation and powder.

Eyes: brush on your eye-shadow. Draw a thickish line of grey eye pencil along the rim of your socket and smudge it slightly. Then, paint a line of liquid eyeliner along your top eyelashes.

Glue false eyelashes on to your upper eyelids (see page 24 for the method). Then draw in false eyelashes underneath your eyes with black eye pencil. Put on several coats of mascara.

Lips: cover them with foundation, then put on your lipstick.

Colour co-ordination charts

Look up your skin and hair colour on the charts below, then read across to see some ideas for make-up colours, jewellery and clothes which will suit your colouring.

Daytime

Colouring	Make-up colours	Jewellery	Clothes
Fair skin/brown hair	**Blusher**: tawny pink **Eyes**: sand brown and gold **Lips**: coral	**Natural things** (pp 42-45) in ivory, ochre and caramel.	Casual, sporty clothes in khaki, beige or white.
Fair skin/blonde hair	**Blusher**: peach **Eyes**: cornflower blue and pinky mauve **Lips**: sugar pink	**Pretty things** such as necklace (p 48), bangles and hair comb (p 47) in pinks, soft blues and lemon yellows.	Soft, feminine clothes in pastel shades.
Freckled skin/ red hair	**Blusher**: amber **Eyes**: golden brown, rust and sage green **Lips**: burgundy	**Natural things** (pp 42-45) in brick red, ivory and sage green.	Strong ethnic prints in green, rust and black.
Black skin/dark hair	**Blusher**: burgundy **Eyes**: rose and navy **Lips**: wine red	**Classic things** such as speckled jewellery (p 55) in navy and white or burgundy and white.	Sophisticated, classic clothes in cream, navy or burgundy.
Brown skin/ dark hair	**Blusher**: mauve **Eyes**: blue and mauve **Lips**: oyster pink	**Pretty things** such as rose brooches and earrings (pp 50-51) in pink, pale peach, green and yellow.	Crisp, white or pink shirt or shirt dress.
Olive skin/dark hair	**Blusher**: copper **Eyes**: moss green and gold **Lips**: chestnut	**Natural things** (pp 42-45) in terracotta, caramel and ochre.	Sporty cotton jersey clothes in cream, soft brown or mustard.

Evening

Colouring	Make-up colours	Jewellery	Clothes
Fair skin/brown hair	**Blusher**: tawny pink **Eyes**: grass green, apricot and blue **Lips**: rich red	**Crazy things**, such as toy box necklace and dolly earrings (p 59) in bright, primary colours.	Bright, cotton jersey clothes in colours such as pillar box red, day-glo orange, electric blue, yellow and green.
Fair skin/blonde hair	**Blusher**: peach **Eyes**: grey or soft brown **Lips**: peach brown	**Classic things**, such as enamel-painted necklace, bangle and earrings (p 54) in black and silver.	Classic, crew or polo neck sweater in camel, black or cream.
Freckled skin/ red hair	**Blusher**: dusky pink **Eyes**: tawny pink and plum **Lips**: raspberry	**Pretty things**, such as marabou bangles and earrings (p 49) in soft pink or cherry red.	Soft, fluffy sweater or sweater dress in cream, plum or grey.
Black skin/dark hair	**Blusher**: brick red **Eyes**: yellow and orange **Lips**: shocking pink	**Bright things**, such as papier mâché necklace, bangles and earrings (pp 37-39) in yellow, orange and black.	Striking dress or top in a plain, bright colour such as orange, yellow or green.
Brown skin/ dark hair	**Blusher**: golden brown **Eyes**: tawny gold **Lips**: brick red	**Classic things**, such as enamel-painted necklace, bangle and earrings (p 54) in black and gold.	Bold, ethnic print clothes in colours such as black, rust, gold and sage green.
Olive skin/dark hair	**Blusher**: burgundy **Eyes**: french navy and plum **Lips**: burgundy	**Classic things**, such as rhinestone brooches, cuff-links and rings (pp 56-57).	Black sweater or sweater dress to show off the rhinestones (or you could wear them on a black beret as on p 57).

MAKE-UP & JEWELLERY

PART TWO   JEWELLERY

Felicity Everett & Carol Garbera

Illustrated by Lily Whitlock and Chris Lyon

Designed by Camilla Luff

Edited by Janet Cook

Contents

About jewellery

The jewellery in this book is stylish, simple and cheap to make.
Part two is divided into five sections, each showing a different
style of jewellery. You might want to make all the things in
one section, or choose a few items from each.
Since there is something to suit most tastes, you
can make jewellery as presents, or even to sell.
You can see the five styles below.

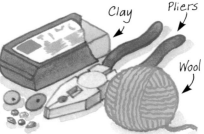

Bright Things

Natural Things

Pretty Things

Classic Things

Crazy Things

Things you need

Clay
Pliers
Wool

You can see what materials, tools and equipment you need to make the jewellery on pages 62-63 (you may already have some of them). Try to work tidily – it is easy to spoil a piece of jewellery while working on a messy surface.

Instructions

Clear instructions, illustrated step-by-step, explain how to make each item. All the basic skills, such as making papier mâché or clay beads, are clearly labelled, so you can refer back to them if you get stuck.

Design hints

The book shows certain colours and designs for each piece of jewellery, but you can choose your own. Design hints, in coloured boxes like this, suggest simple ways of adapting the jewellery.

Choosing what to make

Each section has a patterned border at the top of every page so you can easily see where it starts and ends. Every item of jewellery is coded so you can tell how long it takes and what it costs to make (see the key opposite).

Key

▲	up to 2 hours	● very cheap
▲ ▲	up to 1 day	●● cheap
▲ ▲ ▲	1 to 2 days	●●● quite cheap
▲ ▲ ▲ ▲	2 days or more	●●●● more expensive

Bright things

In this section you will find bold jewellery, painted in bright, abstract patterns. Most of it is made from papier mâché, which takes a few days to dry. But if you are patient, you will be rewarded with stunning results. Below are some of the things you can make.

Papier mâché
bangle

Paper
earrings

Papier
mâché brooch

Papier mâché
necklace

Paper
necklace

This jewellery looks especially striking if you wear it with **Razzle dazzle** make-up. See page 28 to find out how to put it on.

Making papier mâché

The quantities listed below are for the earrings, necklace, brooch and bangle. Make less if you only want to make one or two items.

For the paste: 1 ¼ litres (about 2 ¼ pints) warm water to 250g (8-10oz) plain white flour. In addition you need two or three old newspapers, a washing up bowl and a spoon.

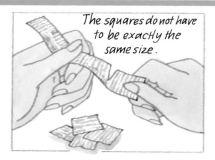

The squares do not have to be exactly the same size.

Tear the newspaper into 2cm (¾in) squares. To make the paste, gradually mix water into the flour in the bowl, until there are no lumps.

Then stir in the newspaper and leave it to stand for two or three hours, until the paper goes really soft. The papier mâché is then ready to use.

Papier mâché necklace ▲▲▲▲ ●●

You will need:
½ ltr (about ¾ pt) papier mâché
poster paints, fine paint-brush and jam jar
paper varnish and varnish brush
3 or 4 4mm* knitting needles OR
16 to 20 cocktail sticks
Vaseline
about 1¼ m (1¼ yd) metallic cord and a darning needle
old potato
sandpaper
sticky tape

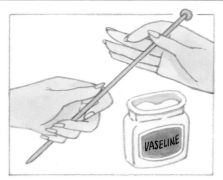

If you want to make chunky beads, cover the knitting needles with a thin coat of Vaseline. For finer beads, do the same with cocktail sticks.

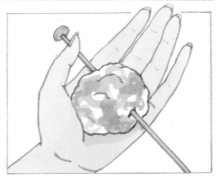

Take enough papier mâché in your hand to make the size of bead you want. Press the knitting needle or cocktail stick into it, as shown.

Then mould the papier mâché around the knitting needle, squeezing out the spare paste. Smooth it with your fingers until it is the shape you want.

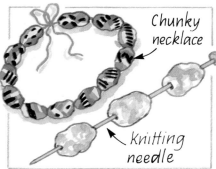

Chunky necklace

knitting needle

To make a chunky necklace, you will need to make 12 papier mâché beads 5cm (2in) long. You should be able to fit three on each knitting needle.

Fine necklace

Cocktail sticks

To make a finer necklace, make 16-20 beads 4cm (1½in) long. Make each one on a cocktail stick. You can see how to paint them over the page.

*English size 8, or US size 5.

Bright things 2

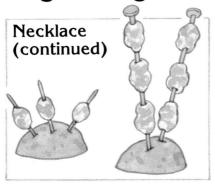

Necklace (continued)

Cut a potato in half and stick the knitting needles or cocktail sticks into it, as shown. Leave the beads to dry* like this for three to five days.

Sanded even.

When the outsides are dry, slide the beads off the needles and leave them for a day, so that the middles dry. Then sandpaper the ends to improve the shape.

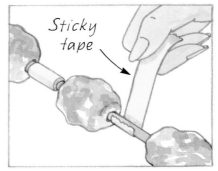

Sticky tape

Now thread the beads back on to the needles or sticks and wind sticky tape around the needle in between each one, to keep them separate.

Painting your beads

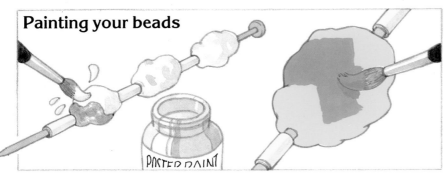

POSTER PAINT

Paint two coats of white poster paint on each bead. This evens out the surface, making it easier to paint your pattern on later. Leave them to dry.

Keeping your hand as steady as you can, paint a pattern on each bead. Begin with the lightest colour you want to use and let one dry before using another.

Below are some ideas for patterns and colour combinations.

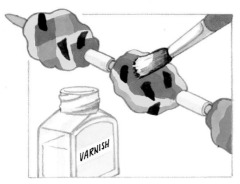

VARNISH

When the paint is dry, keep the beads on the needles, and brush on a thin coat of paper varnish. Let it dry, then brush on a second coat.

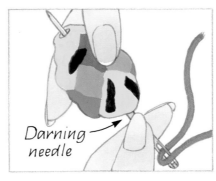

Darning needle

When the varnish is dry, slide the beads off the needles and thread them on to your metallic cord with a darning needle. Tie the ends in a secure bow.

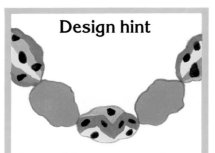

Design hint

You could paint some of your beads with a plain colour that matches the patterned ones. Then make a necklace by threading up alternate plain and patterned beads.

*The beads will dry more quickly in summer than in winter. Do not try to dry them over direct heat.

Papier mâché bangle ▲▲▲▲ ●

You will need:

¼ ltr (about ½ pt) of papier mâché
poster paints, fine paint brush
and jam jar
paper varnish and varnish brush
70cm (about 2ft) 0.8mm (¹⁄₃₂in)
wire (or 30 amp fuse wire*)
an old plate
Vaseline
wire cutters or blunt scissors
sandpaper

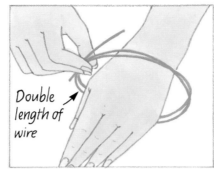

Double length of wire

Cut** a length of wire long enough to fit twice around the widest part of your hand with a bit to spare. Twist it into a circle to make your bangle base.

Cover an old plate with a thin layer of Vaseline. Using this as your work surface, mould handfuls of papier mâché roughly around the wire base.

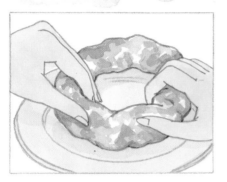

When you have covered all the wire, mould the papier mâché into a smooth, even shape. Leave it in a warm place for several days until it feels dry.

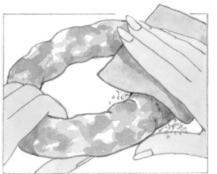

Sandpaper the edges smooth. Then paint it as for the beads (you do not need to paint a pattern on the inside). When dry, brush on two coats of varnish.

Two finished bangles.

Papier mâché brooch ▲▲▲▲ ●

You will need:

¼ ltr (about ½ pt) of papier mâché
for two brooches
poster paints, fine paint brush
and jam jar
paper varnish and varnish brush
an old plate
Vaseline
brooch back
strong glue

Working on a greased plate, shape the papier mâché into a disc with a flat base, about 6cm (2½in) in diameter and 1cm (½in) thick. Leave it to dry.

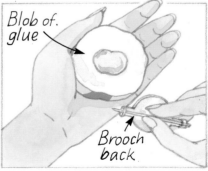

Blob of glue

Brooch back

Then paint it as for the beads. Paint the back a plain colour. Varnish it when the paint is dry. When the varnish is dry, glue a brooch pin on the back.

*You can buy fuse wire from hardware shops.   **Use wire cutters or old scissors to cut it with.   39

Bright things 3

Papier mâché earrings ▲▲▲ ●

You will need:

2 big papier mâché beads (see page 5)
1 pair clips (with loops for dangly earrings) or ball hooks
40cm (about 16 in) of 0.6 mm (¼ in) wire (or 15 amp fuse wire)
2 wooden beads, 1cm (½in) across
strong glue
wire cutters or old scissors

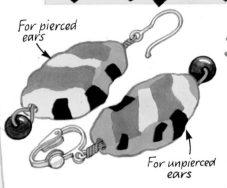

For pierced ears

For unpierced ears

You can make these earrings for either pierced or unpierced ears. Use clip-on attachments for unpierced ears and ear hooks for pierced ears.

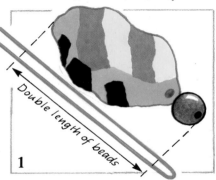

Double length of beads

1

First measure your beads. Double this measurement and add 5cm (2in). Use the wire cutters to cut two pieces of wire this long, one for each earring.

Making paper beads*

The quantities below will make three bracelets, two necklaces and a pair of earrings.

Six sheets of coloured paper (such as cover paper), 52 × 78cm (20 × 30in), 150ml (¼pt) of wallpaper paste, an old washing up bowl, a 3¾mm** knitting needle, a thin paste brush, clear paper varnish, Vaseline and a ruler.

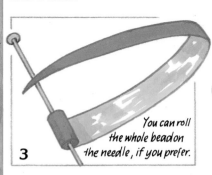

You can roll the whole bead on the needle, if you prefer.

3

Roll the strip around the knitting needle a few times to form a hole, then slip it off and roll by hand. Make all the beads like this.

Making big, tapered beads

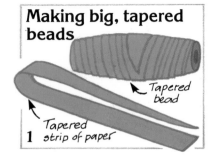

Tapered bead

Tapered strip of paper

1

Cut a strip of paper about 3cm × 78cm (1in × 30in). Then cut it to a point from half-way along, as shown. This makes it taper at each end.

Making small, straight beads

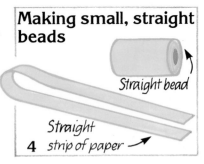

Straight bead

Straight strip of paper

4

Cut straight strips of paper 1½cm × 78 cm (½in × 30in). Then paste them, roll them up and varnish them, as for the big beads.

Wallpaper paste

2

Coat a knitting needle with a thin layer of Vaseline. Then thinly brush some of the wallpaper paste over one side of the strip of paper.

Varnishing both types of bead

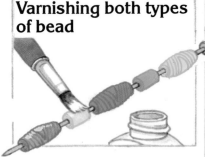

When the paste is dry, put the beads on to the knitting needle, five at a time and varnish them. Let the varnish dry, then varnish another batch.

*You can see how to adapt these beads on page 48.   **English size 9, or US size 4.

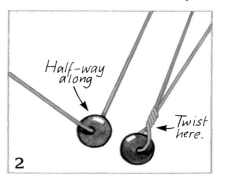

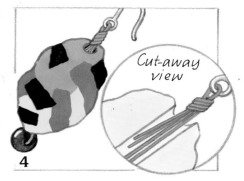

2 Push a small wooden bead to the middle of one of the lengths of wire. Bend both ends around the bead, and twist them together a few times.

3 Thread both ends of wire through your papier mâché bead. Then thread one end through the hole in the ear hook or clip, as shown above.

4 Wind the second end of wire around the first. Then dab a tiny blob of glue on the spare ends of wire and push them back into the earring.

Paper necklace and bracelet ▲▲ ●●

You will need:

For the necklace: 26 big rolled paper beads, OR 16 big and 16 small beads
about 1m (1yd) of elastic cord
paper varnish and varnish brush

For the bracelet: about 5 big beads and 3 or 4 small beads
about 25cm (10in) of elastic cord
paper varnish and varnish brush

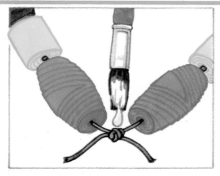

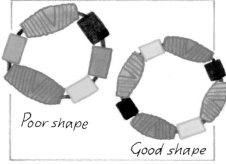

To make a necklace, thread the beads on to the elastic, varying the colours and sizes. Knot the elastic securely, then seal it with a blob of varnish. Trim ends.

You make the bracelet in the same way, but you need to arrange the beads evenly so that you end up with a good circular shape, as shown above.

Paper earrings ▲▲ ●●

You will need:

6 big paper beads and 2 small paper beads

4 wooden beads, 1cm (½in) across

1 pair kidney wires or clips (with loops for dangly earrings)

2 lengths of 0·6mm (⅟₆₄in) wire (or 5 amp fuse wire) 30cm (12in) long

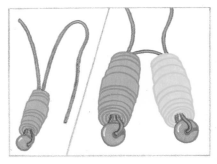

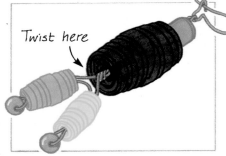

Thread a wooden bead, then a big bead half-way along the wire and thread one end back up the big bead. Thread on two more beads, as shown, doubling the wire through the big bead again.

Twist the wire at the top of the two big beads, then thread the double wire through a third big bead and a small bead. Thread on a kidney wire and finish as for the papier mâché earrings.

Natural things

The jewellery on the next four pages is all based on primitive shapes and natural, earthy colours. It is made from clay and wooden beads, corks, seeds and leather thongs. Clay beads are quite easy to make. Once you have mastered the basic techniques, you can experiment with different shapes and textures of bead. Combined with plain wooden beads and stained corks, they can look very dramatic.

In this section, you will see how to make the items of jewellery shown here.

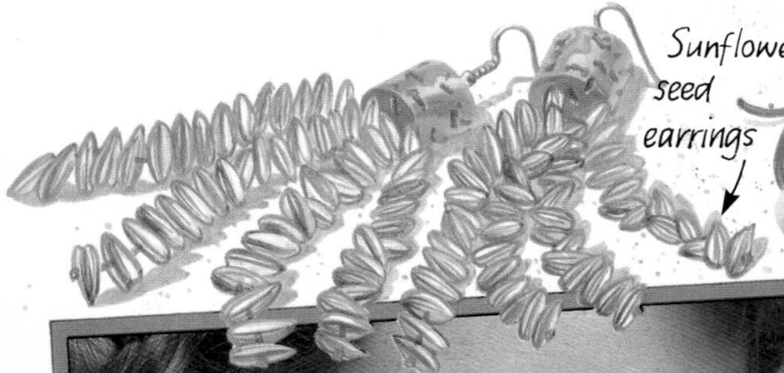

Sunflower seed earrings

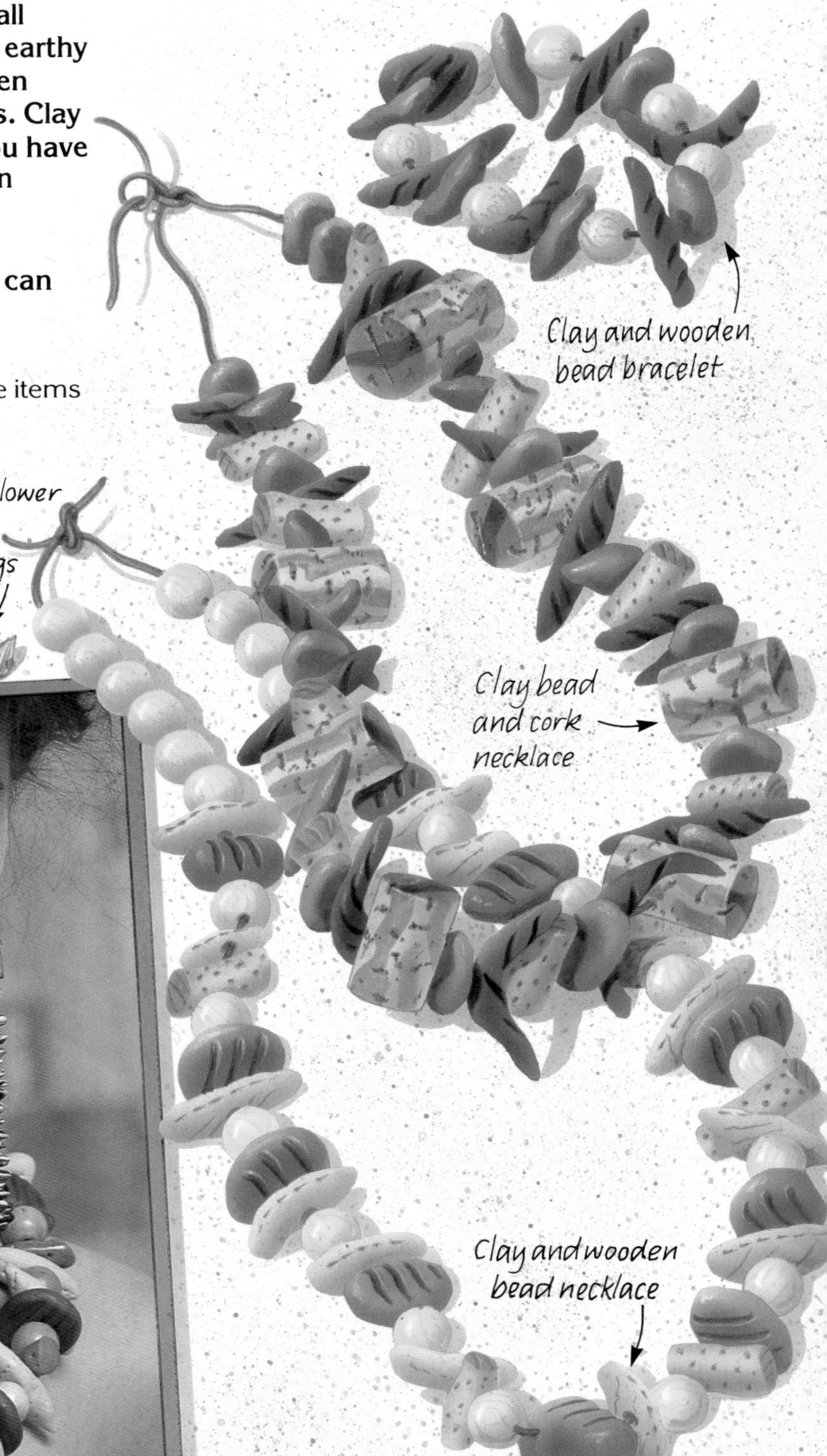

Clay and wooden bead bracelet

Clay bead and cork necklace

Clay and wooden bead necklace

Natural look make-up looks very good with this jewellery. See page 18 to find out how to put it on.

About self-hardening clay

You can buy self-hardening clay from most craft shops. Some makes come in a range of different colours*, others come in just one colour and can be painted afterwards. Self-hardening clay is easy to mould and dries to a hard, smooth finish when baked in the oven. Read the instructions on the packet before you begin.

Different shapes of bead

Below are the various designs of bead used for the jewellery shown opposite. You can design your own beads if you prefer, making patterns with implements such as clay modelling tools, coins with serrated edges, or pencils.

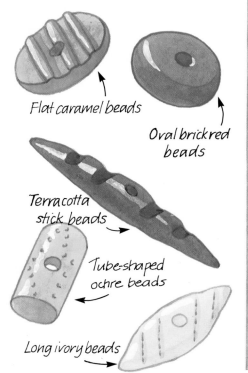

Flat caramel beads

Oval brick red beads

Terracotta stick beads

Tube-shaped ochre beads

Long ivory beads

Making clay beads

You will need seven packets of clay in different colours to make all the jewellery in this section. Choose earthy colours such as terracotta, ivory and ochre, for a natural look.

You will also need a 4mm** knitting needle, an old serrated knife and an old fork, clay varnish, a baking tray and some tin foil.

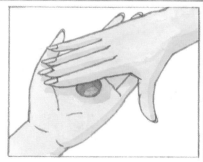

Roll a small piece of clay in your hands until it is soft. Then mould it into a bead. There are some ideas for bead shapes on the left.

The serrated edge makes a good pattern.

Gently pierce the centre of the bead with your knitting needle. Before taking it off, mark patterns on it with the knife blade or fork prongs.

For the flat, caramel beads only, carve a pattern first, using the prongs of the fork. Then pierce the centre of the bead with the knitting needle.

Check oven temperature given on the packet.

Cover a baking tray in tin foil. Space the beads out on it. Heat the oven to 100-130°C (200-250°F) and bake for 10-20 minutes.

When the beads are cool, varnish them, letting one side dry before doing the other. On page 44 you can see what you can make with the beads.

---

*E.g. *Fimo*. See addresses on page 63. **English size 8, and US size 5.

Natural things 2

Clay bead and cork necklace ▲▲▲ ●●

You will need:
1 packet of brick red clay
1 packet of terracotta clay
½ packet of ochre clay
7 new wine bottle corks*
bottle of wood stain
and fine paint brush
clay varnish and varnish brush
1m (1 yd) leather thonging
old serrated knife
old fork
pointed skewer
baking tray and tin foil

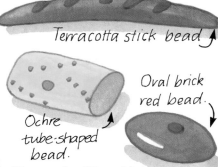

Terracotta stick bead

Ochre tube-shaped bead.

Oval brick red bead.

First make 17 oval brick red beads, 18 terracotta stick beads and 8 tube-shaped ochre beads, following the instructions on the previous page.

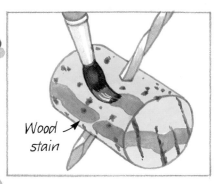

Wood stain

Carefully pierce the corks horizontally with the skewer, as shown. Paint on the wood stain in wavy lines. Leave the corks to dry, then varnish them.

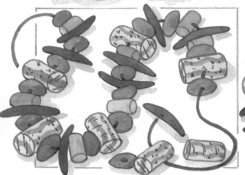

When the varnish is dry, thread the corks and the clay beads on to the thonging. Arrange the corks near the front, to give your necklace a good shape.

Tie a secure knot here.

Check your finished necklace for length. If it is too long, take off some of the beads from each end. Finally, tie the thonging in a secure knot.

Design hint

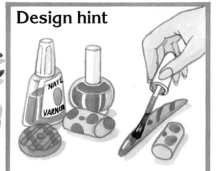

NAIL VARNISH

You could use nail varnish to paint patterns on your beads. You do not need to varnish them again if you decide to do this.

Clay and wooden bead bracelet ▲▲▲ ●●●

You will need:
7 wooden beads about 2cm
(¾ in) across
½ packet of brick red clay
½ packet of terracotta clay
about 22 cm (9in) of elastic cord
clay varnish and varnish brush
baking tray and tin foil
4 mm knitting needle
old serrated knife
old fork

Stretch elastic to seal knot.

Make six oval brick red beads and six terracotta stick beads (turn to page 43 to see how). Thread them on the elastic, knot it, then seal it with varnish.

Some finished bracelets.

*You can buy these from shops selling home-made wine kits and from chemists.

Sunflower seed earrings ▲ ●

You will need:
100g (4oz) sunflower seeds
1 reel grey button thread
sewing needle
2 new wine corks
1 bottle of wood stain
fine paint brush
1 pair ball hooks or clips (with loops for dangly earrings)
sharp knife
pointed skewer
old towel or rag
varnish and varnish brush

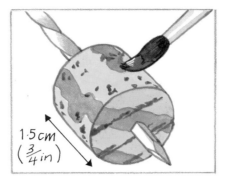

1.5cm (¾in)

Cut a piece of cork, 1½cm (¾in) deep. Pierce it vertically, as shown, then paint on some wood stain. Soak the seeds in water for an hour.*

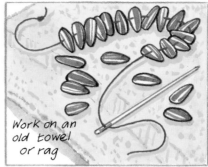

Work on an old towel or rag

Drain the seeds. Then knot one end of a piece of thread. Thread 22 seeds on to it, then thread it through the cork and cut it off 15cm (6in) from the top.

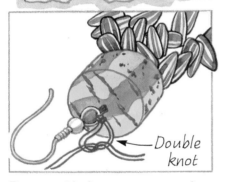

Double knot

Repeat with three more strands, threading them through the same piece of cork. Tie the strands on to the earring wire in a double knot.

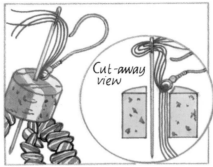

Cut-away view

Thread each end on to a needle and push them into the cork, as shown. Seal the knot above the cork and the knots at the base of each strand with varnish.

A finished pair of earrings

Clay and wooden bead necklace ▲▲▲ ●●●●

You will need:
1 packet ivory clay
1 packet caramel clay
½ packet ochre clay
25 wooden beads, about 2cm (¾in) across
1m (1yd) leather thonging
Clay varnish and varnish brush
4mm knitting needle
old serrated knife
old fork
baking tray and tin foil

Make 13 long ivory beads, 5 flat caramel beads and 5 ochre tube-shaped beads (see page 43). Thread them on to your thonging starting with six wooden beads.**

Finish off with six wooden beads. Adjust the length of your necklace by taking off some of the wooden beads at each end, if it is too long. Tie the thonging in a knot.

*So that they do not crack when threaded.   **This makes the necklace more comfortable to wear.

Pretty things

On the next six pages you can find out how to use rolled paper beads, ribbon-type yarn, fabric flowers, marabou and coloured clay to make a collection of delicate jewellery in soft pastel shades.

In this section, you will find out how to make the items shown below.

Multi-strand necklace

Rose brooch

Rose brooch

Floral hair comb

Marabou earrings

Rose earrings

Ribbon-covered bangles

Ribbon-covered bangles

You will need:

50g (2oz) ball of ribbon-
type yarn* (1 ball of yarn
covers at least 3 bangles)
old plastic bangles ½cm (¼in)
to 1cm (½in) thick and about
7cm (2¾in) in diameter
strong glue
small elastic band
scissors

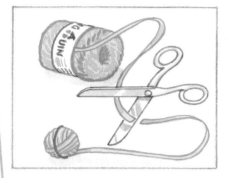

Cut about 3m (3½yd) of yarn off the main ball and wind it into a smaller ball. Unwind 30cm (1ft) of it to start with, and put an elastic band round the rest.

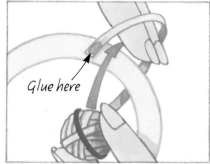

Glue here

Glue the end of the yarn on to the bangle. Then take the yarn, in a loop, round the outside edge of the bangle and up the middle, as shown above.

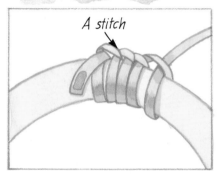

A stitch

Pass the ball of yarn through the loop and pull it until a stitch forms. Carry on like this, pushing each stitch close to the one before.

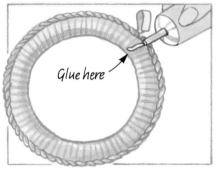

Glue here

When the whole bangle is completely covered, cut off the spare yarn, leaving a 1cm (½in) end. Glue this firmly to one side of the bangle.

Design hint

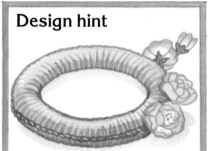

You can adapt the basic design to suit your taste. For example, you could glue a few fabric flowers on to the bangle. Then wind your yarn round to cover the stalks.

Floral hair comb

You will need:

about 2m (2yd) ribbon-type
yarn
plastic hair comb
strong glue
spray of small silk flowers**
scissors

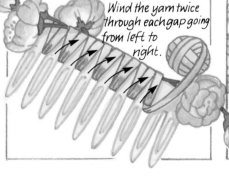

Wind the yarn twice through each gap going from left to right.

Glue flowers along the top, outside edge of the comb. Glue one end of the yarn to the back of the bar and wind it round, to cover the stalks, as shown.

Wind the yarn only once through each gap going from right to left.

Then wind the yarn back to the beginning again, diagonally, as shown, to cover any gaps. Cut off the spare yarn and glue the end to the back of the comb bar.

*Such as *Pingouin Ruban.*   **You can buy these from department stores.   **47**

Pretty things 2

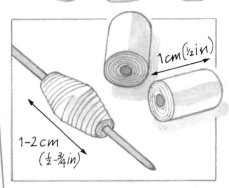

Multi-strand necklace ▲▲▲ ●●●

You will need:
6 sheets strong white paper, about 30×20cm (12×8in)
¼ litre (about ½pt) wallpaper paste and fine paste brush
paper varnish and varnish brush
poster paints and fine paint brush
cocktail sticks and Vaseline
3m (3½yd) bead thread, sewing needle and screw clasp
88 glass beads ¾cm (⅝in) across

Cut the paper into 87 strips about 1cm (½in) × 30cm (1ft). Roll them into beads (see page 40) using a greased cocktail stick to form the hole.

Thread beads back onto cocktail sticks to paint them.

Thin some poster paint with an equal amount of water and paint patterns on the rolled beads. Let each colour dry before using another. Varnish them when dry*.

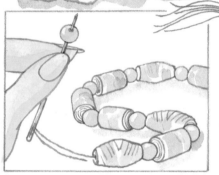

Thread the needle with 1m (40in) of thread. Working on a flat surface, so the beads stay on, thread 31 rolled beads on to it, alternately with 30 glass beads.

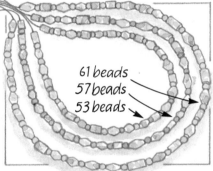

61 beads
57 beads
53 beads

Make two more rows in the same way, using 29 paper beads and 28 glass beads for the middle one and 27 paper beads and 26 glass, for the short one.

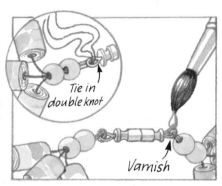

Tie in double knot

Varnish

Thread two glass beads on to all three row ends. Then tie the ends on to one half of the clasp and varnish the knot to make it strong. Repeat at the other end.

Hoop earrings ▲▲ ●

You will need:
pair of silver earhoops 3½cm (1½in) across

4 glass beads (or more if you prefer) ¾cm (⅝in) across

2 rolled beads (or more if you prefer).

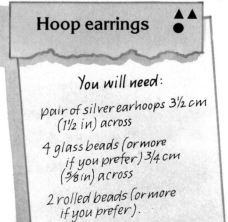

Thread beads on to this end

Paint and varnish the rolled paper beads, as for the necklace. Thread a glass bead, then a rolled bead, then another glass bead on to each earring.

Design hint

You can use any combination of beads, threaded on to the ear hoops. Try two paper beads and one glass bead, or just one big paper bead.

*They will take about an hour to dry thoroughly.

Marabou bangles

You will need:

plastic bangle at least 8cm (3in) in diameter
about 1m (1yd) of marabou*
1 reel of matching thread
sewing needle
about 1m (1yd) ribbon-type yarn (or ribbon ½cm [¼in] wide)
strong glue
scissors

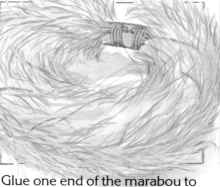

Glue one end of the marabou to the bangle. Bind it with thread, as shown. Wind the marabou evenly around the bangle and secure the other end as before.

Glue one end of your yarn to the bangle and wind it tightly round the join, until it is all used up. Glue the end neatly in place on the inside of the bangle.

Marabou Earrings

You will need:

2 wooden curtain rings 6cm (2½ in) across, with eyelets
8m (9yd) ribbon-type yarn (or ribbon ½cm [¼in] wide) cut into 2 equal lengths
40cm (16in) marabou cut into 2 equal lengths
1 reel matching thread
sewing needle
1 pair of kidney wires
strong glue

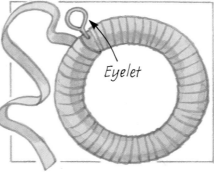

Eyelet

Glue one length of yarn next to the eyelet of one of the curtain rings. Wind the yarn tightly round the ring, as shown. Leave 15cm (6in) free at the end.

Bind together the ends of a piece of marabou with thread. Then glue it on to your curtain ring, so the join aligns with the neck of the eyelet.

Wind the spare 15cm (6in) of yarn around the neck of the eyelet to cover the join, then around the curtain ring. Glue the end to the back of the ring.

Pull the marabou loop through to the front of the curtain ring and fluff it up. Thread the ring on to your earring wire. Repeat for the other earring.

This jewellery looks good worn with a fluffy jumper.

*Marabou is stork's down. You can buy it from haberdashery shops and department stores.

Pretty things 3

Rose brooches and earrings

You can make these delicate rose brooches and earrings from self-hardening clay.* The ones shown here were made using clay which was already coloured, but you can also buy a plain clay and paint and varnish it after baking. Use thinned poster paint and the varnish which the clay manufacturer recommends.

Posy and garland brooches.

Earrings.

Making the roses

Half a packet each of pink, pale peach, green and yellow clay is enough to make all the things shown on these two pages. You could use what is left over to design your own rose jewellery.

The roses are made up from flowers, buds and leaves. They are quite fiddly to make but the results are well worth the effort.

Bud

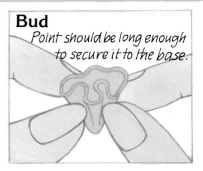
Point should be long enough to secure it to the base.

Make a small ball of peach clay, then flatten it into a disc about 1mm (¹/₁₆in) thick. Gently pinch the centre into a point.

Leaf

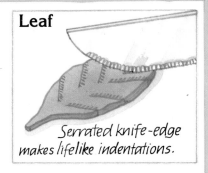
Serrated knife-edge makes lifelike indentations.

Roll out some green clay about 1mm (¹/₁₆in) thick. Use your knife to cut out a leaf about 2½cm (1in) long. Mark it with the knife, as shown.

Flower

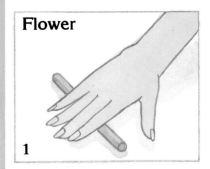
1

Break off a small piece of pink clay and mould it until it is soft. Roll it into a sausage about ½cm (¼in) wide and 12cm (5in) long.

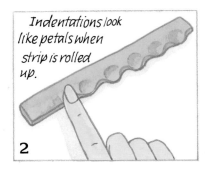
Indentations look like petals when strip is rolled up.
2

Flatten the sausage to make a strip about 1cm (½in) wide. Indent the edges with your fingertip, as above, to make the petals.

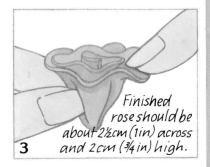
Finished rose should be about 2½cm (1in) across and 2cm (¾in) high.
3

Gently roll up the strip of clay, pinching one edge and opening out the other, to make a rose. Put a dot of yellow clay in the centre.

50 *You can find out more about self-hardening clay on page 43.

Clip-on earrings ▲▲▲ ●●●

You will need:

self-hardening clay in pink,
pale peach, green and yellow
baking tray and tin foil
old rolling pin
old serrated knife
clay varnish and varnish
    brush (optional)
2 clip-on earring backs
strong glue
sharp knife

Make two flowers, two buds and six leaves. Then make two discs, 2mm (⅛in) thick, which will cover your earring clips. Gently press the roses on to them.

Bake the earrings, as it tells you on the packet. For a shiny effect, varnish the tips of the petals, when they are cool. Then glue on the earring backs.

Brooches ▲▲▲ ●●●

You will need:

self-hardening clay in pink,
    pale peach, yellow and green
old rolling pin
old serrated knife
baking tray and tin foil
clay varnish and varnish
    brush (optional)
brooch pins
strong glue
sharp knife

Posy brooch

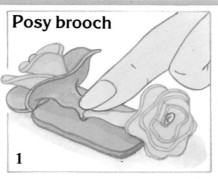

1

Make three flowers, two buds and seven leaves. Make a base about 4cm × 3cm × ½cm (1½in × 1¼in × ¼in). Gently press the roses on to it, as shown.

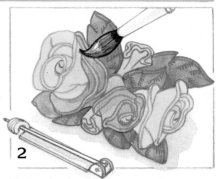

2

Bake the brooch, as it tells you on the packet. When it is cool, varnish the tips of the petals if you want a shiny effect. Then glue on the brooch pin.

Garland brooch

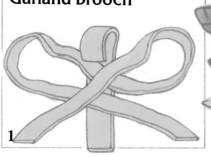

1

Cut a strip of clay ¼cm × 19cm (⅛in × 7½in). Make it into a figure of eight. Cut a strip 4cm (1½in) long and wrap it around the first, to make a bow.

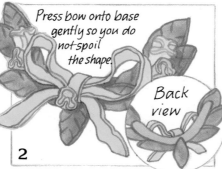

Press bow onto base gently so you do not spoil the shape.

Back view

2

Roll a V-shaped base. Make five buds and eight leaves and press them on to it, with the bow in the middle, as shown. Finish off as for the posy brooch.

Design hint

You can use any arrangement of roses that you wish, and vary the size of the base. The brooch above is made on a long, narrow base.

Classic things

The jewellery in this section is sophisticated and stylish. You can see how, with a coat of paint, old beads and bangles can be transformed into dazzling jewellery. You can also find out how to make glamorous jewellery out of clay and rhinestones and how to make some stunning party earrings from glittery net.

Here are some of the items in this section.

Net earrings

Enamel-painted necklaces

Button clip-on earrings

Enamel-painted bangles

This jewellery looks good worn with a simple crew or polo neck sweater.

Net earrings for pierced ears ▲ ●

You will need:
20cm (8in) glitter-patterned net
1 reel strong, matching sewing thread
sewing needle
1 pair ball hooks
2 beads about 2cm (3/4in) across
4 beads about 1cm (1/2in) across
4 gold washers about 1cm (1/2in) across
sharp scissors

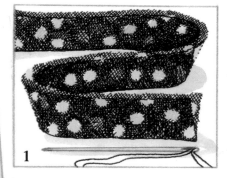

Cut the net into two strips 10cm (4in) × the width of the net*. Fold one strip in half lengthwise. Thread your needle with a double length of thread.

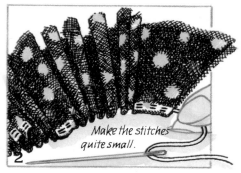

Make the stitches quite small.

Starting with a few stitches on top of one another, loosely sew along the fold, through both layers of net. Pull the thread end so the net begins to gather.

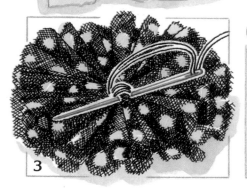

Gather the net up until the ends overlap to make a circle. Then sew across the centre to close up the hole. Leave 20cm (8in) of spare thread on the needle.

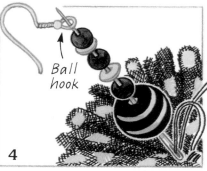

Ball hook

On to the spare thread, thread a large bead, then three small beads alternately with two washers. Finally, thread on your ball hook.

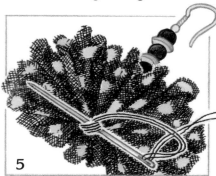

Now thread the needle back through each bead and washer to the under-side of the net and oversew to fasten off. Make a second earring in the same way.

Net clip-on earrings ▲ ●

You will need:
20cm (8in) glitter-patterned net
1 reel strong, matching sewing thread
sewing needle
sharp scissors
2 clip-on earring backs
strong glue

Make two net circles, as above. Fasten off neatly on one side of each circle. Then firmly glue an earring clip in the centre of each one to cover the stitching.

Design hint

You could make either type of earring from plain net, and then decorate them, by glueing or sewing on sequins or tiny beads.

*If your net is very stiff, you may need to use less than the full width of the fabric.

Classic things 2

Enamel-painted necklace ▲▲▲ ●●●●

You will need:
37 beads about 2cm (¾ in) across and 38 flat beads* about 1cm (½ in) across
3m (3½ yd) strong bead thread and darning needle
2 pots contrasting enamel paint, fine paint brush, white spirit, jam jar, and old newspapers
clear varnish and varnish brush
2 pairs 2¼ mm knitting needles**
sticky tape and an old potato

Stick knitting needles into potato halves while the beads dry

Thread the large beads on to knitting needles. Wind sticky tape in between. Holding each knitting needle over newspaper, paint the beads all over.

When this coat of paint is dry (after about six hours), paint patterns on the beads in the contrasting coloured enamel. Leave to dry as before.

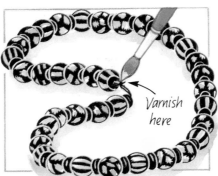

On to a double length of knotted thread, thread a flat bead, then a round one, then another flat one. Continue until all the beads are used up.

Varnish here

Tie the ends of the thread together in several double knots and cut off any left-over thread. Seal the knots with a blob of varnish.

Design hint

This necklace looks good in any colours. You could paint an old bangle to match it and make some earrings (see below) for a matching set.

Button clip-on earrings ▲▲▲ ●●

You will need:
2 round buttons about 2½ cm (1in) across, with metal shanks
pliers
2 pots contrasting enamel paint, fine paint brush, white spirit, jam jar, and old newspapers
1 pair clip-on earring backs
strong glue

Shank

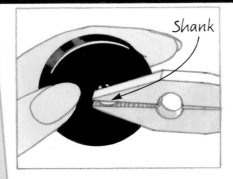

Twist the shank of the button with the pliers until it breaks off. Repeat with the other button. Working on newspaper, paint both buttons all over.

Earring back

Leave the buttons to dry for six hours. Then paint patterns on the front of the buttons, in a contasting paint colour. When dry, glue on the earring backs.

*You could use small buttons instead.   **English size 13, US size 0.

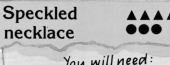

Speckled necklace

▲▲▲▲
●●●

You will need:

300 beads about 1cm (½ in) across
2 pots contrasting enamel paint,
 fine paint brush, white spirit,
 jam jar and old newspapers
stiff bristled paste brush
2 x 4 row end bars
3m (3½ yd) strong bead thread, 1 reel
 ordinary sewing thread and
 sewing needle
pliers and scissors
strong glue
jump ring and bolt ring

Before you start

The jewellery on this page is patterned by splattering it with white paint. This is fun to do, but can be rather messy so it is best to do it out of doors, on a fine day, or in a garage or workroom. You should put down lots of old newspaper first.

You might have to re-touch patchy areas later

Thread up the beads loosely on ordinary thread*. Then paint them on one side with your base colour. When dry, turn them over and paint the other side.

Stiff bristled paste-brush

Mix some contrasting paint with an equal amount of white spirit in a jam jar. Splatter your beads with it, as shown. Leave them to dry. Turn them over and repeat.

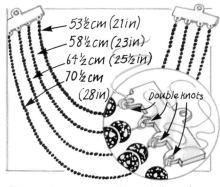

53½ cm (21 in)
58½ cm (23 in)
64½ cm (25½ in)
70½ cm (28 in)
Double knots

Thread your needle with bead thread and make up four rows of beads the above lengths. Tie the ends to the loops of the end bars, as shown.

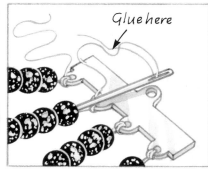

Glue here

Rethread the needle. Run glue along the thread and push it back through a few beads to secure it. Repeat for each strand at either end.

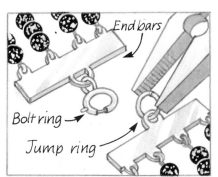

End bars

Bolt ring

Jump ring

Using pliers to open and close them, fit a jump ring through the loop on one end bar and a bolt ring through the loop on the other one.

Design hint

You can decorate a bangle to match this necklace, and make some matching button earrings (see left) which can be splattered in the same way.

Speckled jewellery

---

*If you rest them on a flat surface, they won't fall off as you thread them.

Classic things 3

About rhinestones*

Rhinestones without mounts

Mounts

Rhinestones with mounts

Imitation jewels made of glass or plastic are called rhinestones. Some have metal mounts which you can either clip on to the back of the stone, or use separately for extra decoration.

Rhinestone brooch ▲ ●●●●

You will need:
about ½ packet self-hardening clay (see page 11)
baking tray and tin foil
tweezers
ruler
sheets of clean, white paper
brooch back
rhinestones for decoration
strong glue

Roll a ball of clay 4cm (1½in) across. Working on clean paper, flatten it into a disc about 6cm (2½in) across and ½cm (¼in) thick, using a ruler**.

Use tweezers to arrange the rhinestones on the brooch, as shown. Then gently press them into the clay with your finger tip, without touching the clay.

Put the brooch on your baking tray and bake it in the oven, following the instructions on the packet of clay. When it is cool, glue on a brooch back.

Design hint

Initial brooch   Small brooch

You can make brooches in practically any shape and size and vary the patterns you make with the rhinestones.

Rhinestone key-ring ▲ ●●●

You will need:
about ¼ packet of self-hardening clay
ruler
sheet of clean, white paper to work on
baking tray and tin foil
rhinestones and mounts
tweezers
key-ring fixture

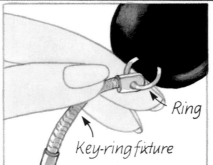

Ring

Key-ring fixture

Roll a ball of clay about 2½cm (1in) across. Push the key-ring fixture firmly into it as shown, so that the ring is half buried in the clay.

Flatten the ball into a disc about 4½cm (1¾in) across. Then decorate it with rhinestones and mounts, and bake it, as for the brooch above.

Rhinestone cuff-links

You will need:

about ¼ packet of self-hardening clay
ruler
sheet of clean, white paper to work on
baking tray and tin foil
pair of cuff-link backs
rhinestones and mounts
tweezers

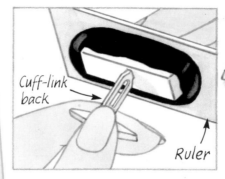

Roll a piece of clay the size and shape of your cuff-link back. Flatten it with a ruler on to the cuff-link back, so it extends ¼cm (⅛in) all round.

Make the other cuff-link in the same way. Decorate both of them with rhinestones and rhinestone mounts and bake them, as for the brooch opposite.

Rhinestone rings

You will need:

about ½ packet self-hardening clay (makes two or three rings)
baking tray and tin foil
ruler
sheet of white paper to work on
flat ring backs
rhinestones and rhinestone mounts for decoration
strong glue

Designing a round, flat ring

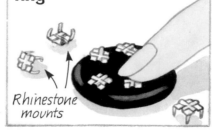

Roll a ball of clay 1½cm (¾in) across. Flatten it with a ruler into a disc about 2cm (1in) across and ½cm (¼in) thick. Decorate it as for the brooch.

Designing a dome-shaped ring

Roll an oval piece of clay about 2cm (1in) long and 1cm (½in) high. Flatten one side of it with a ruler. Decorate it as for the brooch opposite.

Finishing the rings

Bake the decorated clay in the oven, following the instructions on the packet. When it is cool, glue the clay on to the ring backs, as shown.

Design hint

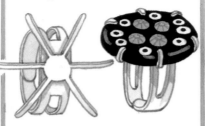

Instead of using a flat ring back, you could mount the round, flat ring on a claw-shaped ring back, so that the tips of the claws stick out round the edge.

Rhinestone jewellery.

Crazy things

The jewellery in this section is bright and fun to wear. You can find out how to make woolly pom poms with oddments of left-over wool, and adapt them to make various kinds of jewellery.

There are also lots of ideas for making crazy jewellery out of children's toys.

Here are some of the things you will find on the next three pages.

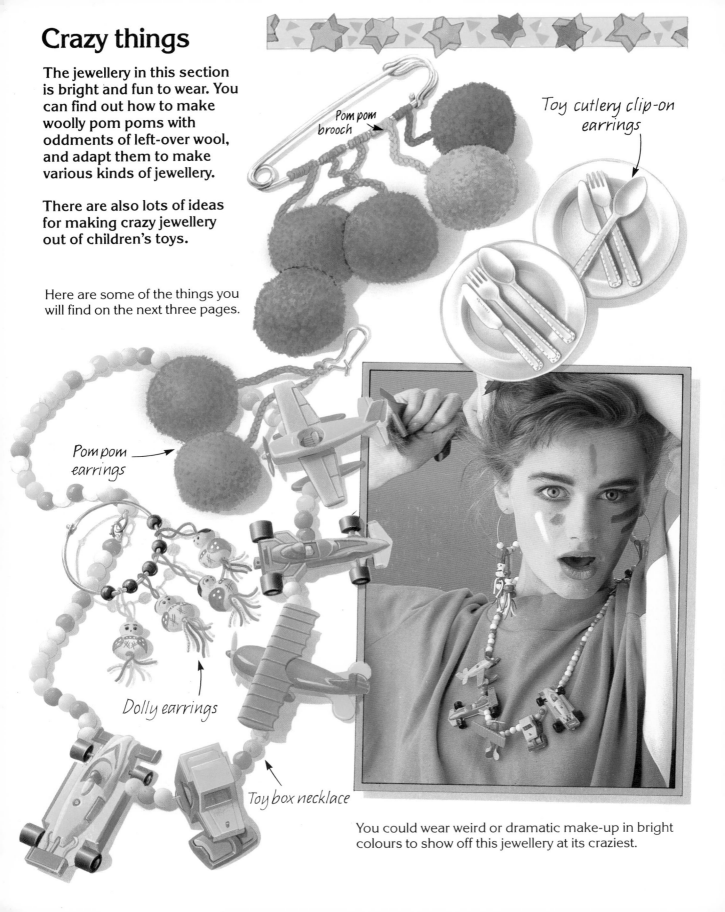

Pom pom brooch

Toy cutlery clip-on earrings

Pom pom earrings

Dolly earrings

Toy box necklace

You could wear weird or dramatic make-up in bright colours to show off this jewellery at its craziest.

Toy box necklace ▲ ●●●

You will need:

5 plastic toys such as miniature cars, trains and planes, plastic animals, dolls house furniture etc

82 plastic beads about 1cm (½in) across

about 1½m (5ft) strong bead thread

sewing needle

jump ring and bolt ring

scissors

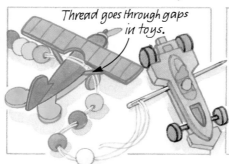

Thread goes through gaps in toys.

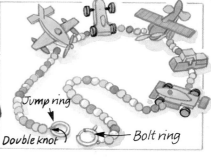

Jump ring

Double knot

Bolt ring

Thread your needle with double thread. Leaving 10cm (4in) at the start, thread on 33 beads*. Thread up the toys, with about four beads between each one.

Thread up 33 more beads, leaving 10cm (4in) of thread at the end. Tie on a bolt ring at one end and a jump ring at the other and trim off the spare thread.

Cutlery brooch and clip-on earrings ▲ ●●

You will need:

3 sets of miniature plastic or metal cutlery and plates**

strong glue

clip-on earring backs

brooch back

scrap paper to work on

Glue cutlery where you like

Glue the cutlery firmly on to the plates. Glue earring clips on to the backs of two plates and a brooch back on to the back of a third and leave them to dry.

Cutlery earrings and brooch.

Dolly earrings ▲ ●

You will need:

1 pair of ear hoops about 3½cm (1½in) across

8 little wooden dolls (or Christmas decorations) with hanging loops

10 plastic beads about 1cm (½in) across

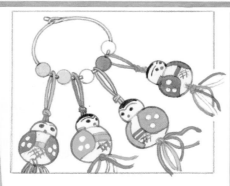

Thread up four wooden dolls (or Christmas decorations) on each ear hoop, alternately with five plastic beads. Start and finish with a bead.

Design hint

Pearl and pig necklace

Doll's shoe brooch

You can use all sorts of things to design your own crazy jewellery. The basic techniques stay the same. Above are some ideas.

*Work on a flat surface so the beads stay on the thread.　　**You can buy these from some toy shops.

Crazy things 2

Making a woolly pom pom and chain

Dotted lines show how to find centre of card square.

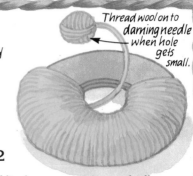

Thread wool on to darning needle when hole gets small.

You need spare double knitting wool, a piece of card 7cm (3in) square, a pencil, sharp scissors, a crochet hook and a darning needle.

1 On double card, draw a 3½cm (1¼in)* diameter circle. Draw a 2cm (¾in) diameter circle in the middle of it. Cut them out to make two rings.

2 Wind your yarn into a ball which will fit through the centre hole. Then tie the end on to the two rings and wind the yarn around them.

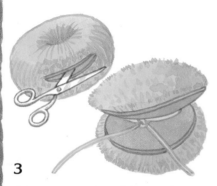

Loose slip knot

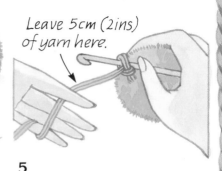

Leave 5cm (2ins) of yarn here.

3 When the hole is full, cut the yarn between the rings. Part them and tie a piece of yarn 75cm (30in) long, tightly around the middle.

4 Tear off the card rings and fluff out the pom pom. Tie a loose slip knot in the yarn ends, as close to the pom pom as you can make it.

5 Put your crochet hook through the slip knot as shown. Hold the crochet hook and pom pom in your right hand and the yarn, as shown, in your left.

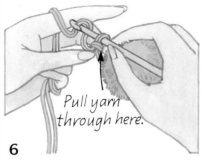

Pull yarn through here.

End loop. Pull to fasten off.

6 Holding the slip knot in your left hand, catch a loop of double yarn with the crochet hook and draw it through the loop of your slip knot.

7 Carry on until the chain is the length you want it. Then hook the yarn through the end loop and pull tight. Leave the ends 18cm (7in) long.

Design hint

You can make a two-tone pom pom. First work a few rounds of one colour, then change to another colour.

Pom pom earrings ▲▲ ●

You will need:

2 pom poms with chains 5cm (2in) long

2 pom poms with chains 7cm (3in) long

scissors

darning needle

pair of kidney wires

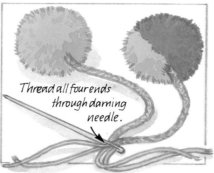

Thread all four ends through darning needle.

Make two pom poms with 5cm (2in) chains and two with 7cm (3in) chains. Thread the yarn ends of one long and one short chain on to a darning needle.

Kidney wire goes through here.

Neatly darn the four yarn ends into the chains, as shown. Thread a kidney wire through the join at the top. Make another earring in the same way.

Pom pom brooch ▲▲ ●

You will need:

5 pom poms with chains about 7cm (3in) long

darning needle

kilt pin (or a giant safety pin) about 6cm (2½in) long

scissors

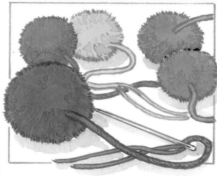

Make five pom poms, each with a chain about 7cm (3in) long. Thread the spare yarn at the ends of one chain on to your darning needle.

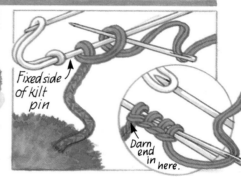

Fixed side of kilt pin

Darn end in here.

Stitch the yarn ends over the fixed side of the kilt pin. Then stitch for another 1cm (½in), as shown. To finish off, darn the ends into the crochet chain.

Repeat with the other four pom poms. When you have stitched them all on, the metal on the fixed side of the kilt pin should be covered with wool.

Design hint

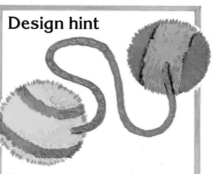

You can turn pom poms into almost anything. For instance you can make a hair bobble by stitching together two big pom poms on long chains.

The finished pom pom jewellery.

Tools, equipment and materials

Here you can find out about the things you need to make the jewellery. If you have problems finding the more unusual items, you may be able to order them by post. Many companies have a mail order service and there are some useful addresses opposite.

Findings

The metal components needed to make jewellery (known as findings) can be bought from specialist craft shops (see addresses opposite).

For earrings

Pierced ears:

Kidney wire

Metal ear hoop

Ball hook

Unpierced ears:

Clip (with loop for dangly earrings).

Screw (with loop for dangly earrings).

Clip on earring back.

Screw-on earring back.

For necklaces

Screw clasp with loops.

Bolt ring and jump ring.

Jump ring and hook.

End bar.

For brooches

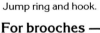
Brooch pin

Brooch back

For key-rings, cuff-links and rings

Cuff - link backs

Ring back

Key ring fixture

Wire (for earrings and bangles)

0.6mm ($\frac{1}{64}$in) wire (or 15 amp fuse wire) for earrings.

0.8mm ($\frac{1}{32}$in) wire (or 30 amp fuse wire) for papier mâché bangles.

Equipment

Jam jar		White spirit	
Old rags		Newspapers	
Baking tray		Tin foil	
Cardboard box (to keep everything in).		Card	
Old rolling pin		Sticky tape	
Old washing-up bowl		Old spoon	

Tools

Ruler		Tape measure	
Wire cutters or blunt scissors		All purpose scissors	
Sharp knife		Small pliers	
Cocktail sticks		Knitting needles	
Sewing needles		Darning needle	
Paste brush		Fine paint brushes	
Varnish brush		Tweezers	
Pencil		Crochet hook	
Old serrated knife		Old fork	
Pointed skewer		Sandpaper	

Materials

Self-hardening clay (from art and craft shops).	**Strong paper**, such as coated cartridge, or cover paper (from art shops).	**Clear paper varnish** (from art shops). Alternatively, use clear nail varnish.
Clay varnish (from art shops). Use the type recommended for the brand of clay you use.	**Wooden curtain rings** (from furnishing departments).	**Buttons with shanks** (from haberdashery shops).
Kilt pins (from haberdashery departments).	**Ribbon-type yarn** (from wool shops). Sold under different brand names.	**Sequins** (from haberdashery shops). These are shiny pieces of decorative plastic.
Rhinestones (from craft shops and haberdashery departments).	**Marabou**, or stork's down (from haberdashery departments).	**Fabric flowers** (from haberdashery departments). Can be silk or synthetic.
Children's toys (from toy shops) and novelties from Christmas crackers.	**Old or broken jewellery**	**Plain or glitter-patterned net.** You can buy this from haberdashery shops.
Sunflower seeds (from health food stores and pet shops).	**Woodstain** (from D.I.Y. shops).	**Strong glue** which is recommended for wood, metal and plastic.
Poster paint and enamel paint	**Oddments of wool**	**Wine corks** (from shops stocking home wine-making kits).

Beads (from craft shops, haberdashery departments and shops selling jewellery findings).

Plastic beads

Wooden beads   Metal washers   Glass beads

Thread (from haberdashery departments and shops selling jewellery findings).

Elastic cord →
Strong bead thread (polyester, or nylon)
Leather thonging →
Thick metallic cord →

Useful addresses

Jewellery findings

Creative Beadcraft Ltd,
Unit 26, Chiltern Trading Estate,
Earl Howe Rd, Holmer Green,
High Wycombe,
Buckinghamshire, England.

Hobby Horse Ltd,
15-17 Langton Street, London
SW10 0JL, England.

Beadshop,
43 Neal Street, London
WC2H 9PJ, England.

Rio Grande Albuquerque,
6901 Washington NE,
Albuquerque,
New Mexico 87109, USA.

Watts International
Findings Company Inc.,
6024 South Memorial Drive,
Tulsa, Oklahoma 74145, USA.

John Bead Corporation Ltd,
21 Bertrand Avenue,
Scarborough, Ontario,
M1L 2P3, Canada.

Johnston Silvercraft Ltd,
579 Richmond Street West,
Toronto, Ontario,
M5V 1Y6, Canada.

Supercraft Emporium,
33 Moore Street, Perth, WA
6000, Australia.

Johnson Matthey Ltd,
114 Penrose Road,
Auckland 6, New Zealand.

Jewelcraft,
51 Unley Road, Parkside, 5063,
South Australia.

Fimo clay
Available from branches of
W.H. Smith in the UK.

For details of availability
elsewhere, please contact:

Staedtler (Pacific) Pty. Ltd,
P.O. Box 576, Dee Why, N.S.W.
2099, Australia.

Connelly Bros. Ltd,
7 Falcon Street, P.O. Box 496,
Parnell, Auckland 1,
New Zealand.

Accent Import Export Inc,
460 Summit Road, Walnut
Creek, Ca. 90210, U.S.A.

Dee's Delights Inc,
3150 State Line Road,
Cincinatti, North Bend, Ohio
45052, U.S.A.

Index

Photographer **Simon Bottomley**

For Part One:

Session co-ordinator **Saskia Sarginson**
Stylist **Sara Sarre**
Make-up **Louise Constad**
Hair **Tony Collins** for **Joshua Galvin** and **Louise Constad**
Models **Mickey** at **Synchro**, **Akure** at **Look**, **Emma Campbell** and **Louise Kelly** at **Select**

For Part Two:

Stylist **Carol Garbera**
Make-up **Wendy Saad** at **Joy Goodman**
Hair **Carlo Braida** at **Schumi**
Model **Louise Kelly** at **Select**

The following companies kindly contributed clothes and accessories for the photographs:

Liberty, Goldie, Fenwicks, Corocraft, Katherine Glazier and Extras (both at Hyper Hyper), Alexis Lahellec, Oui, Hyper Hyper, Molton Brown, The Yarn Store and Neal Street East. All room sets by Habitat.

The following kindly gave permission to reproduce the photographs on these pages:

Page 10 left, Elle/Transworld
Page 10 right and centre and page 11 right, Jacinte/Transworld
Page 11 left, Fashion Fair
Page 11 centre, Seventeen at Boots

First published in 1987 by Usborne Publishing Ltd, 20 Garrick Street, London WC2E 9BJ, England. Copyright © 1987 Usborne Publishing Ltd.

The name Usborne and device are Trade Marks of Usborne Publishing Ltd. All rights reserved.

Printed in Belgium.

No part of this publication may be reproduced, stored in any form or by any means mechanical, electronic, photocopying, recording, or otherwise without the prior permission of the publisher.